All contents ©2015 by Jenny Ashford, Stephen Mera and Bleed Red Books.
Cover design by Jenny Ashford.
Interior photos © Stephen Mera.

All rights reserved. No part of this publication may be reproduced, distributed, or transmitted in any form or by any means, including photocopying, recording, or other electronic or mechanical methods, without the prior written permission of the publisher, except in the case of brief quotations embodied in critical reviews and certain other noncommercial uses permitted by copyright law.

Printed in the United States of America

THE ROCHDALE POLTERGEIST

A TRUE STORY

Jenny Ashford and Steve Mera

FOREWORD

When you spend so much of your time writing horror fiction, I suppose you shouldn't be surprised when your real life begins to take some strange turns.

When I published *The Mammoth Mountain Poltergeist* with my partner and former poltergeist focus Tom Ross, in March of 2015, I didn't have much of an inkling of the doors it would open. I admit I didn't know a great deal about the paranormal before that time, other than Tom's story and the handful of cases I researched for the book, and I also admit that, to this day, I'm still intensely skeptical about a great deal of the phenomena. During the course of promotions for the book, being interviewed by believing hosts of various paranormal radio shows and podcasts, I maintained my skeptical stance, though naturally I wholeheartedly believe the Mammoth Mountain case to be genuine. But then my skepticism took yet another hit when I met Steve Mera.

Tom actually met him first, after hearing about him in conjunction with the extraordinary case this book describes. He approached Steve on Facebook, telling him about our book and his own experiences, and the two struck up an online friendship. Tom then sent a copy of *The Mammoth Mountain Poltergeist* to Steve in the UK. Steve read it, and was impressed enough that he wrote a glowing review of it in *Phenomena Magazine*, the publication put out by Manchester's Association of Paranormal Investigation & Training (MAPIT).

MAPIT was originally formed in 1974 to specifically research UFO reports, but later expanded to encompass other paranormal phenomena. Their website proclaims that they specialize "in confidential investigations for city councils, housing associations, businesses, police departments, CID and corporate companies since 1996." Their stance is one of rigorous scientific investigation, and the fact that Steve, their chairman, shared this rationalist approach was important to both Tom and to me.

During Tom and Steve's discussions, it came to light that of the many thousands of cases Steve had been involved in over the thirty-plus years of his career, he had only seen a handful that he believed displayed some truly inexplicable phenomena. Tom asked him about these, and Steve obliged by describing two cases that he felt contained the best evidence for what we would call "paranormal," or specifically poltergeist, phenomena. Tom then suggested I detail these cases in book form. Steve readily agreed, and thus began my involvement with the book you now hold in your hands.

※

Over the next few weeks, Tom and I interviewed Steve over Skype from his home in Manchester, and he told us of his riveting investigations into poltergeist territory. He came across as eminently credible, rational, and level-headed on the subject of the paranormal, and of the Rochdale case in particular. His protocols for conducting investigations were well-thought-out and very stringent, taking into account the possibility of fakery and natural phenomena being mistaken for supernatural. He told us in all seriousness that before the Rochdale investigation, he had never seen anything on any of his previous cases that had shaken him, or caused him to question the career path he had chosen.

The incidents at the little house in Rochdale, however, were quite another matter. "Up to that point," he said, "I was quite happy to be interested in the paranormal because I really hadn't experienced much. Until I did. And then I was thinking, 'Oh God, do I really want to continue with this? I don't know.'"

Readers, of course, can judge for themselves the veracity of the case described herein. I have written an account of the events at Rochdale exactly as Steve Mera described them to me, with no exaggeration or embellishment. Steve was also gracious enough to share his case notes and photographs with me, and some of them have been reproduced in these pages. Additional information relevant to the case was also gleaned from the MAPIT website, the original newspaper reports of the Rochdale incident, and summaries in other paranormal books and websites that mentioned the case in question.

I extend my most heartfelt thanks to Steve for spending so much of his time and energy on this project, and subjecting himself to my and Tom's relentless assault of questions. I'd also like to thank Tom for facilitating our meeting and setting the whole thing into motion.

Steve would like to extend special thanks to Peter, Alicia, Val, Vic, and Carole.

CHAPTER ONE

The Scientific Establishment of Parapsychology (SEP) keeps its offices within the larger organization of Manchester's Association of Paranormal Investigation & Training (MAPIT), an organization originally created in 1974 to investigate UFOs, and later, other anomalous phenomena including hauntings, strange creature sightings, and other mysterious doings in Manchester, England and surrounding areas.

It was July 23, 1995, and the UK was in the midst of a historic heat wave. Other than that, though, it was a perfectly ordinary day. Parapsychologist and MAPIT chairman Steve Mera was in his office as he usually was, and nothing at all seemed amiss. There was, in fact, little to suggest that this day would serve as the beginning of a months-long ordeal that would end up turning Steve's life and skeptical world-view upside down, and eventually cause him to question the very profession he'd spent decades cultivating.

A secretary entered Steve's office and handed him that day's copy of the *Manchester Evening News*, opened to one particular article. The headline read, "Spooky Spills Scare Family From Home," and Steve chuckled, not so much at the alliterative turn of phrase, but at the accompanying photo.

It showed a family of three staring up at a profoundly water-damaged ceiling, with the man holding a mop up to the water stain, as though vainly attempting to dry it off. Beneath yet another photo of a small, unassuming bungalow made of corrugated aluminum, the short article detailed the ongoing woes of the Gardner family, who had been plagued by unexplained outpourings of water that had ruined much of their furniture. The family explained that they had contacted the Rochdale Council on several occasions over the preceding year, but no apparent source of the water could ever be found.

Wife and mother Vera Gardner speculated that the disturbances could possibly be supernatural in nature, caused by either a poltergeist or the spirit of her dead husband, who she thought may have been "displeased" that she had remarried. The family told the paper that they had also contacted the priest at their local church, who had performed a blessing on the house, but to no avail.

Steve reread the article with interest. Reasoning that since the family had gone to the press about the disturbances after a reported ten months of experiencing them, he assumed that the council were unable to pinpoint a prosaic cause for what the family claimed was happening. He contacted the Rochdale City Council the very next day to ask about what was going on.

The council confirmed that the Gardner family consisting of Vera Gardner, her second husband Jim, and her 34-year-old daughter Jeanette, from her first marriage—were tenants of a council property on Foxholes Close, and had complained on several occasions of extensive water damage in the home; the source of the water could not be located. The council were evidently operating on the assumption that the family were purposely causing the disturbances in order to be moved to another property, which was apparently not an unheard-of tactic with other families. Steve, curious about the family's claims in the newspaper article, left his information with the city council and asked them to get in touch if they wanted him to conduct an investigation. He then thought no more about it.

Two days later, though, the Rochdale Council contacted Steve at his office and asked him if he would like to attend a meeting where the disturbances at the Foxholes Close property were going to be discussed. At this point, the council were evidently at their wit's end, and willing to call in a paranormal investigation team to look into the reported disturbances, since their own investigations had not turned up any obvious causes for the incidents the family had been reporting. Steve agreed, and when the time of the meeting came, he attended with two of his fellow investigators. Two members of the city council were also present.

At the meeting, the council representatives basically repeated what Steve already knew: that they were at a loss to discover what could be causing the disturbances in the Gardner home, barring some kind of purposeful damage done by the family themselves. The council were eager to forestall any further publicity about the case, since any more negative press could potentially damage their ability to rent other properties.

To this end, they were willing to enlist MAPIT's services in order to get to the bottom of the situation and determine if there was any deception going on. If none could be found, or if the cause was suspected to be paranormal, they welcomed suggestions as to what could be done to help the family, by either attempting to stop the disturbances, or simply by having the family relocated. Steve and his team agreed to take on the case, and made plans to interview the family at the first opportunity.

Foxholes Close is a small cul-de-sac in the market town of Rochdale, which lies about ten miles north-northeast of the Manchester city center. The street consists of perhaps a dozen small bungalows that were among those built at the behest of Winston Churchill after the Second World War, to address Britain's housing shortage. Most of the homes on Foxholes Close, including the Gardners', were small and entirely pre-fab, constructed of aluminum and measuring less than seven hundred square feet.

As Steve approached the Gardner home with his three-vehicle entourage, he lamented that this case would not have the luxury of confidentiality that he was used to on most of the other cases he worked on with MAPIT. The Gardners' troubles had already appeared in the papers, after all, and the street was so small and closely-built that neighbors were already well aware of what had been going on at the home for the previous several months. Steve ruefully pictured curious onlookers pressing their noses to the windows from the neighboring houses as the vans converged on the street. The publicity leading into this case would be a challenge, but as always, Steve's main concern was the safety and well-being of the family he was striving to help.

Steve was the first to arrive on the Gardners' doorstep, followed by a team of five investigators that included Steve's frequent partners, Alicia Leigh and author Peter Hough. At his knock, the door was opened by a small woman in her seventies, who he recognized from the newspaper photo as Vera Gardner. She greeted him and his team, and then broke down in tears as she stood on the threshold.

"She was trying to talk as she was crying, but she was obviously finding it very difficult," Steve says. "I told her that we were there to help, and that she could just take things in her own time." As this was simply a preliminary interview, Steve's goal for this visit was to simply sit down with the family and get an idea of what exactly they were experiencing, and then take a brief tour around the home to get the initial lay of the land and perhaps derive some clue about what it was they might be dealing with.

The entire team proceeded into the bungalow. The first thing that Steve noticed was a pronounced aroma of dampness, a "wet dog smell." The next thing that caught his eye was the presence of large plastic sheets covering the floors and most of the furniture. Vera explained that the council had provided the plastic sheeting in order to protect what was left of their possessions from the so-far unexplained outpourings of water that had been frequently occurring over the previous months. Vera complained that some of the items in the home had already been ruined by the mysterious water, and that the council had been out to the property on several occasions to try to find a leaky pipe or some other rational cause for the damage, but that they had not been able to find anything amiss with the plumbing on any of their visits.

Steve and his team went into the lounge, their feet crinkling on the plastic. Vera lifted a plastic sheet off the sofa and bid them all sit down. It was then that Jim Gardner, Vera's husband of two years, poked his head out of the kitchen and introduced himself. Jim, a bearded man around the same age as Vera, had long hair tied back in a ponytail, and gave off an aura of friendly, laid-back forthrightness. He offered tea, and Steve and one of the other investigators took him up on the offer. Jim then disappeared back into the kitchen to make it.

Vera sat in a chair across from the sofa, still clearly distraught, but seemingly ready to talk. Steve tried to put her at ease, and asked her to tell them, from the beginning, what she and her family had witnessed during their ordeal. Vera, fighting back more tears at several points, began to tell the story.

CHAPTER TWO

The disturbances had started abruptly, nearly a year before. Vera admitted she had no idea what was going on at first, attributing the phenomena to natural causes, as any normal person would be likely to do.

Steve had noted, on a quick scan of the small home, that there was nothing he could see that would indicate that the family had any interest in the paranormal whatsoever; there were no visible books on the subject, no videos of paranormal films or television shows anywhere in evidence. He also noted that the Gardners seemed a completely normal elderly couple, the kind of people who simply kept their heads down and got on with life; hardly the types who would make up such a fantastic story for publicity. While this was not definitive proof that the family's experiences were genuine, it was a detail that Steve filed away to add to the data he hoped to accumulate about the case.

The first manifestation, Vera explained, had been the spontaneous appearance of water dripping from the ceiling. She had been in the kitchen making sandwiches, when suddenly large droplets of water began falling, as though it was raining indoors. Steve asked her to clarify this: "Where on the ceiling was the water coming from?"

Vera answered simply, "Everywhere."

She went on to say that it was as though a shimmering, perfectly even layer of water had appeared, suddenly and inexplicably, on the ceiling and begun to fall, exactly like a heavy rain shower. She could clearly see raindrops forming in this layer, and gravity carrying them to the floor.

The first time the water fell, a shocked Vera scrambled to cover appliances to protect them from the onslaught. After a few minutes, the strange "rain" stopped as abruptly as it had started, leaving the kitchen drenched, but the ceiling oddly dry, as though the water had simply been absorbed back into whatever unseen pocket it had emitted from. Naturally fearing that a pipe in the loft had burst, Vera contacted the council, who had duly come to the property to check it out.

Council representatives, however, had found the

loft space dry and dusty, with no sign of water there or anywhere else in the home. They further informed Vera that these types of pre-fabricated properties actually contained no water pipes in the loft or ceilings at all, as the water was all drawn up from pipes underground and entered the home through smaller pipes in the skirting boards near the floor. "If water is leaking," they concluded, "then it isn't coming from the pipes." They also pointed out that, due to the heat wave the UK had been experiencing that summer, there had been a hosepipe ban in effect that severely curtailed water consumption around the country.

In the interest of thoroughness, the council also performed a full electrical test on the home, but again found nothing amiss. Unable to find any obvious source for the leaking water, the council shrugged their shoulders and left Vera with an incident form, telling her to document further occurrences, and asking her to contact them again if the incidents continued.

Steve watched Vera closely as she described this first bizarre happening. His extensive background in psychology and his long experience investigating similar cases had given him an insight into the behavior of witnesses to anomalous phenomena of this type. He was fairly confident in his ability to detect when someone was being disingenuous, and could recognize several "tells" that witnesses would often unconsciously display when they were exaggerating what they had seen, or even making it up out of whole cloth.

However, he saw no sign of deception as Vera spoke, noting that she seemed to be reliving the incidents as she described them, as well as reliving the distress she had felt. Steve's faith in her truthfulness was reinforced when Jim reentered the lounge, carrying the teacups. As Jim settled himself in and joined the conversation, Steve noticed that the man's body posture was very open and relaxed, and he gave no sign at all that he was particularly anxious at being caught out. Jim seemed content to let Vera tell the story, as the house on Foxholes Close had been her residence for far longer than he had lived in it, but he also had no hesitation about corroborating her story. "It started about ten months ago when we noticed a damp patch on the wall in the back bedroom, which started to leak," he said. "We got the council in and they searched all through the loft but could not find anything leaking."

At Steve's urging, Vera continued her account. She said that the water had emerged from the ceiling on several occasions hence, and that water had begun appearing on the walls and doors as well, just as suddenly as it had on the first day. "Sometimes the water breaks out in the form of huge droplets covering large areas of the ceilings and will disappear as quickly as it comes," she said.

The water apparently behaved in stranger ways, too. Jim added, "We had what we thought was condensation on the ceiling. It started at one place, then it shot right across the ceiling from corner to corner and even seemed to curve around the ceiling light. It would happen in the bedroom and then stop, only to start in the kitchen.

"I rang the council again, and two men went in our loft while an electrician dismantled the ceiling lights whilst I was sat underneath an umbrella in the kitchen. That's how bad it was. The whole kitchen was wet through, as if it were raining. The council men had no idea what was causing it, and in the heat of desperation they decided to fit a fan in the kitchen window. Some good that did."

Jim then went on to give an overview of the water manifestations over the previous few months. "It finally stopped in the kitchen and started in Jean's front bedroom," he said. "It stayed there for four to five months. It happened every day and was causing a lot of upset in the home. When we decided to move Jean's bedroom to another room, it followed as if it knew. The council workmen came again and brought some detectors. They were looking for condensation. Of course, all pre-fabs will have some condensation, especially during the hot weather, but this was ridiculous."

In every one of these "indoor rain" events, the water droplets had disappeared after a few scant minutes, leaving the surfaces they had emerged from dry as bone. A quick glance at the ceiling in the lounge demonstrated that some trace of the water remained, however; Steve could clearly see hundreds of randomly-spaced brown rings staining the painted wood chip paper, spanning the entire width and length of the ceiling.

※

Several nights after the water manifestations had started, Vera said, events had taken a far more sinister turn. Vera and Jim had been sleeping in their bedroom, situated near the front of the home. At around three in the morning, they had both been awakened by the clear sound of footsteps very close by, as though someone was pacing back and forth across the floor of their room. Jim murmured his assent that he had also heard the footsteps very distinctly, and added an interesting detail. The footsteps, he said, sounded as though a person was walking across a normal bare floor, even though their bedroom floor had been covered with plastic sheeting at the time, to protect the flooring from the intermittently falling water. Steve, remembering the loud crinkling noise that had accompanied his team's foray into the lounge, made a note of this fascinating tidbit.

From there, Vera said, the auditory phenomena had escalated. The footsteps became a nightly occurrence, and were soon joined by strange knockings and scratchings on the walls. Shortly afterward, both Vera and Jim heard the sound of a man's raspy cough emerging from the unused back bedroom, which Vera had previously shared with her first husband. It had been this reoccurring sound, in fact, that had caused Vera to suspect that the incidents were perhaps caused by the spirit of her husband, who had died of a heart attack in that room nine years prior. She speculated to Steve that it was possible her first husband was disturbed that she had remarried, although she had no idea why he would have waited so long to demonstrate his annoyance, if that was the case.

The coughing sound had occurred in Jim and Vera's bedroom as well. "We lay in bed and could both clearly hear someone coughing from the corner of the room," Jim said. "Even though I was a little scared, I did thoroughly check the house and found nothing unusual. We've also smelled tobacco smoke in our bedroom and the smell of licorice as if it was a flavored cigarette paper."

Further bolstering the haunting theory, Vera then claimed that she often heard someone whistling a tune when no one else was present in the house. The sound would occur at random times, and often seemed to be coming from thin air.

After a few days of the water and the sounds, Vera continued, the phenomena had ramped up once again. Small items such as pictures, cups, knickknacks and flower pots began to suddenly shoot off of walls, counters, and windowsills with incredible speed, often shattering to pieces on the floor. This also became nearly a daily occurrence, and all told, the incidents seemed to have no discernible pattern, happening at any time of the day or night without warning or preamble. Jim also noted that on at least one occasion, he had seen the lounge door open by itself, and described some incidents of seeming teleportation of objects: "Things go missing and then turn up in the oddest of places some days later when you're not looking for them," he said.

Steve and his team had simply been listening to Jim and Vera's story, rarely interrupting, merely making notes about all the incidents witnessed so far. It was at this point that the third resident of the home, Vera's daughter Jeanette, entered the lounge. Jeanette, a 34-year-old woman with long straight hair and a striking resemblance to her mother, was introduced to the team, but came across as very introverted, even evasive, and seemingly unwilling to talk. Steve noticed right away that the woman suffered from some type of mental disability, which Vera confirmed, telling the team that Jeanette had a mental age similar to that of a young child.

Inwardly, Steve wondered if Jeanette could perhaps be acting as the inadvertent poltergeist focus, should the phenomena prove to be genuine. Though at thirty-four, Jeanette was clearly much older than the typically pre-pubescent or young teenage poltergeist agent seen in other documented cases, he speculated that her disability could possibly be a factor in this age discrepancy.

After the introduction, Jeanette simply sat in

the lounge and watched the proceedings, evidently wanting to be present but not particularly interested in contributing to the discussion.

※

Following the Gardners' brief rundown of events, Vera and Jim invited Steve and his team to take a tour of the home. As per standard protocol, Steve left one member of the team in the lounge to take photographs and keep an eye on things, while he and the others accompanied the Gardners.

The first stop was Jeanette's room, which was also at the front of the house, across the hall from Jim and Vera's bedroom. Steve noted more plastic sheeting covering the bed and furniture in this room, and saw the same brown water stains marring the ceiling paint. The room seemed perfectly normal otherwise, though as they surveyed the space, Vera made the startling observation that the old clock radio on the nightstand had the tendency to turn on of its own volition, even though it was not plugged in and contained no batteries.

"What do you hear when the radio comes on?" Steve asked.

Vera claimed that there was no music nor any regular broadcast radio sounds, but that there were usually words spoken through the radio, and that often the words were related to the Gardner family in some way. Jim compared the sounds to something one would hear emitting from the radio in a taxi; namely, a few distinct words accompanied by static.

Before leaving Jeanette's room, Jim also informed the team, "This is where the battery almost hit me." Upon being asked for clarification, he said that one day when Jeanette was not at home, he had been walking down the hall past her room. The door had been open, and as he had passed, an AA battery had suddenly flown out of the room, narrowly missing his head and slamming into the wall hard enough to leave a dent in the plaster. Steve examined the area that Jim indicated, and clearly saw a pea-sized indentation in the wall of the hallway.

※

The Gardners then led the team into the back bedroom. This was the room where Vera's first husband had passed away, and was understandably no longer slept in. The bed and dresser were covered in plastic as much of the rest of the home was, there were the expected water stains on the ceiling, and there were boxes stacked here and there, indicating the family were using the room for storage. Seeing nothing otherwise untoward, the group continued the tour.

Moving on to the bathroom, Vera claimed that on most mornings as individual family members were washing up at the sink and preparing for the day, toothbrushes would often shoot upward out of the holder and clatter into the bathtub. The same thing happened with tubes of toothpaste, razors, or other small items placed on the side of the sink. Unusually, this would occur only when someone was in the bathroom at the time to witness it; nothing in the bathroom ever moved when no one was in there, unlike the movements of objects in other rooms of the house, which would occur whether someone was in the room or not.

In the kitchen, where the phenomena had first begun, Vera showed the team several broken teacups and plates she had saved. She said that quite often, when family members were in other rooms of the house, they would hear a crash coming from the kitchen, and upon investigation would find various items of crockery smashed on the floor. This almost always happened when no one was in the kitchen.

Upon opening the door to the next stop, Vera and Jim's bedroom, Vera began to cry again. "This is where I hear HIM," she said, apparently still convinced that the wheezing coughs and whistling she heard were indicative of her first husband's ghost. Steve simply nodded. At this point, as he considered the characteristics of the events the family were describing, he emphatically did not believe that the house was being haunted by a spirit, but rather that the possible phenomena were simply mimicking the expected behavior of a ghost in some instances. He did yet not share his hunch with the family, however.

At this point, the group proceeded back through the hallway on the way to the lounge. Vera mentioned that there were sometimes strange smells in the hallway, but didn't elaborate further. No one present smelled anything unusual at the time, so the entire party returned to the lounge and sat down.

"Other than the vicar," Steve asked, once they were all settled, "have there been any other witnesses to any of the incidents?"

Vera said that two neighbors had been present when objects had broken in the kitchen. She also said that a close friend of Jeanette's who had used to visit the home frequently had been terrified in Jeanette's room by the feeling of something invisible hitting her in the back of the head. The girl was still in touch with Jeanette, and the two still saw each other on occasion, but the friend refused to set foot in the Foxholes Close house after that particular occurrence.

⁂

The MAPIT team had been in the Gardner home for a little more than an hour, and Steve felt they had enough data to proceed with a full investigation. As was standard, he provided the family with an incident form on which they were asked to detail every paranormal occurrence they witnessed, and the time that it had taken place.

He also scheduled a second visit for two weeks' hence. This visit would be far more in-depth, with the investigators bringing all of their audiovisual equipment to see if they could capture any evidence of the phenomena. Steve also gave the family the MAPIT contact information and told them that until the second visit, the team would be on 24-hour emergency response, and the Gardners were more than welcome to call at any time of the day or night if something happened that they were unable to handle.

As the team were taking their leave from the home, Steve did something else that he always did on such investigations: he managed to sneak away from the group and hide a small audio recorder behind the sofa cushions. His motivation for doing this was simply to see what the family would say to each other in the few minutes after the investigators had left. In cases of fakery, he'd found, often the complainants would make statements such as, "Do you think they bought it?" or something similar after they had left, strongly suggesting a hoax and saving the team the trouble of investigating further. Steve didn't think the Gardners were faking, but this bit of craftiness was an essential part of any investigation. He rejoined the team without the family being the wiser.

※

After they had taken leave of the home, the three-vehicle caravan drove off a little way down the street and waited for approximately five minutes. Peter Hough wondered aloud whether the hidden recorder would catch the family in the act, but Steve and Alicia remained silent.

After the allotted time had passed, Steve returned

to the Gardner home and knocked on the door. When Vera answered, he told her he had left a piece of equipment behind, and Vera let him in to fetch it. Recorder in hand, Steve returned to his team.

In the car, as Peter and Alicia looked on, Steve rewound the tape and pressed play. The team heard themselves making their goodbyes, heard the slam as the door closed behind them. And then, just as in previous cases, the family began talking among themselves about the investigators' visit.

Vera's distraught voice came first. "Do you think they'll be able to help us?"

Jim, in his laconic tone that was nonetheless tinged with frustration, answered, "Well, the council didn't believe us. I don't know if they will."

If the Gardners were lying about their experiences, they were evidently doing a masterful job of it.

CHAPTER THREE

Steve didn't hear from the Gardner family at all in the two weeks before the scheduled second visit. Whether this was a good thing or not, he couldn't be sure.

As planned, the MAPIT team packed up their equipment and headed for Foxholes Close on the appointed date. As before, they were warmly welcomed by the family, and offered the obligatory cups of tea.

Once everyone had settled in, Steve asked to see the incident forms he'd left for the Gardners. He saw right away that they were amply filled out; there were two pages of incidents described, and from a cursory glance he could see that the occurrences were still happening daily, and that the times of the happenings seemed to fit no obvious pattern. Vera had reported several similar incidents to the ones she had previously described: water falling from the ceilings and walls, phantom footsteps and coughing, small objects flying off of shelves. She had also noted that the council had returned during the interim for yet another visit, and had again found no evidence of a water leak anywhere, nor any other physical problem that would account for the phenomena occurring in the home.

After perusing the reports, Steve asked if they would have any objection to him looking at the loft space for himself. The loft was accessed through a small hatch in the hallway ceiling, just outside of the bathroom. The family had no objections, and Jim went out back to fetch a stepladder and a flashlight. When he returned, the team trooped down the hall, Jim and the ladder in the lead, Steve bringing up the rear. He remembers that the hallway was very hot; it was well into August at that point, the heat wave was still in full swing, and the small home had no air conditioning.

As they made their way down the hall, Steve was suddenly hit on the right temple by a single drop of water, which had presumably fallen from the ceiling. It was a large droplet, larger than a raindrop. He put his hand to his head and then brought his fingers to his face. It certainly looked and felt like normal water. Saying nothing to the others, he glanced up at the ceiling. It was completely dry, giving no hint as to where it had fallen from. "It seemed very deliberate," Steve says.

He purposely kept the incident from the others, wanting to preclude a mass panic, or any type of "me too" syndrome, common in these types of investigations. "At this point I was just taking everything on board and waiting to see what would happen," he says, stating further that he didn't want to derail the investigation protocol with something that may not have been particularly significant. As they went down the hall, though, he kept a close eye on the ceiling, trying to determine where the single droplet of water may have come from. He saw nothing.

Jim put the stepladder down on the floor and allowed Steve to climb up and open the loft hatch. The loft, when Steve climbed into it, was much hotter than the rest of the house, due to its positioning directly beneath the home's aluminum roof. The loft was also bone dry. Shining his flashlight around, Steve saw absolutely no evidence of water or dampness anywhere, nor even any evidence that water had ever touched anything in the loft. He even lifted the insulation and examined the plasterboard beneath, which was likewise dry as a desert, with no signs of water damage whatsoever. Satisfied that wherever the water was coming from, it wasn't coming from the loft, Steve climbed back down. Jim took the stepladder back outside, and upon his return to the house, joined the group, which had reconvened in the lounge.

For a few minutes, and at Steve's request, Jim and Vera elaborated further on the incidents that had occurred in the two-week period between the investigations, which were mostly more of the same types of occurrences they had reported before.

Suddenly, Jeanette entered the lounge, distraught and almost frenzied. "It's happening again!" she cried.

The entire group—family and paranormal team—leaped to their feet in one body and followed Jeanette into the hallway. Several sets of eyes followed her finger as she pointed to the hallway ceiling.

What they saw was nothing short of astounding. "On the ceiling, there was water," Steve says. "I've never seen anything like it before. I'm looking at it, and I'm trying to visually take it all in."

For the water was behaving in a way that no water should be able to behave. Jim had described a similar incident during the team's first visit, but seeing it with their own eyes was quite a different kettle of fish. "It was as if it had an intelligence," Steve says. The water was moving toward him, at a rate of about a half-inch per second, consistently multiplying as it grew. It shimmered as it went. "It moved intelligently across the ceiling without causing any drips to fall. And it decided to take a path *around* a light fitting in the ceiling, as if the light fitting was in its way and it had to maneuver around it."

Tearing his gaze away from this amazing sight, Steve looked at the two investigators flanking him.

They were likewise transfixed, staring at the ceiling with their mouths hanging open, cameras hanging useless in their limp hands. "Get some photos!" Steve commanded.

The team shook themselves out of their shock, and began snapping pictures. Steve began furiously scribbling notes and making sketches of the way the water was impossibly making its way across the ceiling. "The way it moved was, a little string of water would come out first, and then the rest of the water would move to it," he says. "And then at one point it was coming out like little fingers or spikes, with the rest of the water following it."

Peter later described it thus: "It was as if the ceiling was a floor and someone had thrown a cupful of water across it. It had defied gravity!"

Steve also had the presence of mind, while the water was moving, to retrieve a small plastic sample bottle from his kit. He scooped a bit of the water into the bottle, tightened the cap, put the bottle into a plastic bag, and labeled it with the time and circumstances under which it had been gathered.

The water snaked its way across the ceiling in front of the flabbergasted witnesses for almost five minutes, after which it suddenly stopped moving for about a minute, then seemed to evaporate very quickly back into the ceiling from which it had emerged. Moments later, the ceiling was completely dry to the touch.

Despite the unbelievable phenomena they had all

just witnessed, and the excitement they were all feeling, there was still a job to be done. As Steve went to the bathroom tap to obtain a control sample from the home's normal water supply, Peter Hough climbed up into the attic loft himself to check it. Just as Steve had, he found it dry, dusty, and undisturbed.

The team and the family then met up again in the lounge. Vera told them, "This is exactly what happens. Sometimes water just appears on a wall or on a door, drips down for a few minutes, and then disappears again." Steve and his team were eager to organize a more in-depth investigative visit, one for which they wanted the family to be absent, if at all possible. The obvious reason, Steve explains, is to preclude any possibility of fakery by family members, but the team was also curious to see if the phenomena would occur with none of the purported human agents present, suggesting that perhaps the focus—whoever it was—could affect the phenomena from afar.

Vera could see the logic in this plan, and agreed to stay at her sister's house with Jim and Jeanette whenever the investigators wished to have the house to themselves. As details were being discussed, Jim, who had been standing near the kitchen door, gave a shout.

"Here we go again!"

Steve jumped up and headed for the kitchen, with Vera and the rest of the team right on his heels. When he got there, he was greeted with a sight both amazing and amusing.

Jim was standing in the corner of the kitchen, an umbrella opened over his head. He was grinning.

"It was *raining* in the kitchen," Steve says simply. "I looked up, and I could see that the whole kitchen ceiling had the same effect we'd seen in the hallway: a shimmering, half-inch-thick layer of water. But this time, you could see the water suddenly bulge, form drops, and fall to the floor. This was happening thousands of times, all over the kitchen. They were big droplets, and they were just falling all over everything. I could see our cups with the milk in them, and the water was just dropping in there and bouncing off the milk."

"How often does this happen?" Steve asked.

Jim answered very casually, as if nothing odd was going on at all. "A couple of times a week." He was still smiling, standing under the umbrella he kept in the corner of the kitchen for just such an occurrence.

"This is ridiculous," Steve said. Recalling it now, he elaborates, "My thoughts then were that if this was my house, I'd be rushing around with a mop, but Jim just stood there. The impression I got was that, well, everything's going to get wet, we can mop up later. Jim knew to wait until the episode was over before going into cleaning mode."

As Steve watched the rain incredulously, he was sure he saw a few drops going upward. It was such a strange sight that he thought he might have imagined it at first.

After about a minute, the rain began to slow down, and then it stopped. The kitchen was soaked, as though a heavy rain shower had drenched it for ten minutes or more.

"There was water all over the floor, water all over the worktops, the cups, the sink, my shoulders, my hair. I even had it on my glasses," Steve says. Just as in the hallway, the water disappeared quickly. "Imagine you applied a heater to this water," Steve explains. "It just shrunk like that. And as it shrunk it just became nothing. But you could just see a slight brown ring where the water was. It dried up that fast."

"Oh, me kitchen!" Vera clucked, clearly upset and scrabbling for the mop.

"Don't worry, love, it'll all get cleaned up," Steve said reassuringly.

Jim folded up his umbrella and asked the team to wait in the lounge while he and Vera mopped up the mess and made sure nothing in the kitchen was ruined. The team complied, and after Vera and Jim had got their kitchen back to some semblance of normalcy, they rejoined the crew. Vera told the team that she would be in contact with them shortly to let them know when the family would be out of the house, and the team began making their goodbyes, reminding the Gardners that they still had the emergency contact number they could use at any time. At this point Steve wasn't sure how long the investigation would take, but he knew the communication lines would remain open. They left the home for the second time, still agog at all they had witnessed.

There was no longer any suspicion from any member of the team that the Gardners were faking; everyone had seen the phenomena with their own eyes. The family were completely credible in their accounts, on that there was total agreement. There was definitely something extraordinary going on at Foxholes Close, and Steve and the team wanted to get to the bottom of it.

CHAPTER FOUR

The following day, Peter Hough sent the water samples they'd collected to Northwest Water Laboratories for analysis. They had used Northwest several times in the past, and the lab was known for being one of the most reliable in the country.

Afterwards, the team convened for an informal meeting, studying photos and discussing their ideas as to what might be going on in the Gardner home. What was the nature of the phenomena? How was it manifesting itself in this way? Was it translocational, i.e., would phenomena occur even when the family was not in the home, or would it occur in other locations where the family was? Parapsychologists know that poltergeist infestations are generally focus-based and usually need the agent present to occur, but would this case be different? At this point the team were quite sure that the phenomena was probably not residual—a haunting caused by Vera's ex-husband, in other words—because it seemed to be interactive, but this possibility was not ruled out entirely. Everything was still on the table.

If the Gardners were experiencing a typical poltergeist infestation, they mused, then who was the focus? Jeanette? Even though she was much older than the standard poltergeist agent, her mental disability made her a promising candidate. The team also made a note to check the neighborhood around the Gardner home for any children of appropriate age that might be causing the phenomena, just to cover all the bases.

In the next few days, the team didn't rest on their laurels. Steve delved into the parapsychological literature, looking for similar cases for comparison. While he found several documented poltergeist infestations involving water, this almost always manifested as unexplained puddles on the floor, which dried up unusually quickly, as the water at the Gardner home had.

However, at the time of the occurrences in 1996, he was unable to locate another well-documented case that involved indoor rain or intelligently-moving liquid to the extent it appeared at Rochdale. Of course, there was another well-known case of indoor rain that had begun in 1983, that of Don "Rain Man"

Decker in Pennsylvania, as well as a few others that will be summarized in a later chapter of this book, but in the days before the Internet was widely available, Steve was not privy to information about these cases, which at any rate had not been thoroughly investigated by parapsychologists at the time.

The team also researched the history of the Foxholes Close house, looking for any anomalies in its construction, any reports of unusual activity from previous tenants, or anything else that might have some bearing on the case at hand. They found absolutely nothing to suggest a physical cause for the phenomena; the house had been pre-fabricated in the late 1940s, as had all the other houses on the street, and there was nothing particularly unusual about its construction. The council had no records of previous residents ever reporting strange happenings in the home. The neighbors on either side also didn't raise any particular red flags; on one side was an elderly couple, and on the other was a single mother and her boyfriend. This woman did have a child, but the child did not live there. The team were satisfied that they'd done their due diligence regarding the history of the home, and that physical causes for the phenomena could largely be ruled out.

※

A few days later, Vera called and gave the team the date when the family would be at her sister's house, a date only five days' hence. Steve told Vera that he wanted to consult with the family before they left the home, and asked that they wait there until the team arrived before leaving the house to the investigators. Vera agreed.

When the date arrived, Steve says, "We descended upon the house with all guns blazing." The team consisted of Steve, Peter, Alicia, and two other team members, Carole and Valerie. They trundled into Foxholes Close in three vehicles laden with recording equipment.

The family, as requested, were still in the home. For about twenty minutes, Steve consulted with the Gardners separately, asking them to elaborate on any phenomena that had occurred since the team's last visit. Vera and Jim described similar happenings as those they had reported before, though Vera added that Jeanette had been complaining of being "prodded" by unseen hands, often when she was asleep, but sometimes when she was simply sitting on the sofa watching television. She said that the touches were not hard, and did not leave marks, but that often Jeanette would suddenly jump and claim something was touching her, and that this was very upsetting for her. Steve made a note of this.

After the discussion, the family left the team the keys to the house, told them to help themselves to food and drink, and said they would return at ten o'clock the next morning. They left. "Now we had the premises to ourselves, so this is where the fun starts," Steve says jokingly.

The team brought their video cameras and audio recording equipment into the house and began setting up for the night. "The first thing we did," Steve says, "was get a videoscope. That's what we call it when we take the camera and just do a very slow pan around each room, 360 degrees. We do this so that if there is any movement of objects, we can recheck the videoscope and see where the items have come from and how far they've moved from their original places."

This process took about a half-hour, after which the main camera—a heavy, unwieldy thing common in the days before digital video—was set up in the corner of the lounge, facing the television. "The camera was fitted with a special criss-cross lens," Steve says. "When you look through the camera, it looks as though you're looking through a mesh. Obviously, this is done so that we can calculate distances easily on the grid if objects happen to move on video."

The team then took the standard temperature readings in every room of the house. Though it was summer and still quite light outdoors, dusk was slowly approaching, and the outside temperature was dropping. The rooms of the Foxholes Close home all read completely normal temperatures ranging around the low- to mid-70s Fahrenheit. There was nothing unusual at all in the home, in fact; it was quiet, comfortable, and completely innocuous looking. Steve, for his part, was not really expecting to experience anything untoward, since the family members were not present to "stir up" the phenomena.

As it turned out, he was quite wrong.

※

The team made themselves cups of tea and sat down in the lounge for a chat. "We basically just wanted to sit and relax and monitor the environment, and see what would happen," he says.

For the first hour, absolutely nothing unusual occurred. "It was very quiet; you could hear the birds chirping outside," Steve says. "There was no oppressive atmosphere, no unusual odors, no unusual sounds. It was just a normal environment. Everyone was quite relaxed. We sat there until about nine o'clock, and absolutely nothing happened. We then decided to proceed with a more active investigation."

Per procedure, the team divided into two groups. Each group would spend half an hour sitting in a different room, after which the groups would rotate members and move to other rooms, so that over the course of the night, each investigator would have sat in every room. This was done, Steve explains, to see if certain phenomena would only happen to certain people, or to certain combinations of people.

It should also be noted that, as a precaution, the investigators were wearing no deodorants, perfumes, or hairsprays, so that any strange odors noticed in the home could not be attributed to physical causes. They also kept the lights on in the rooms where this was feasible. "We don't believe these investigations have to be conducted in the dark, or with infrared cameras or any of that," Steve specifies. "We're very aware of the problems that can arise from investigating things in the dark. The psychological reactions, how the brain works, how the eyes work. People tend to go into defense mode in the dark; it's their survival sense. People can see or hear things that aren't really there, or misinterpret things that are there, like shadows in the corners and so forth." As far as possible, the team tried to account for every physical aspect of the environment, so they could be sure that any phenomena they witnessed were truly anomalous. At this point, it was starting to grow dark outside the windows, and the team noted that the temperature in the house had dropped about eight degrees. This was likewise perfectly normal.

For the first rotation, Steve and Alicia dispatched to Jeanette's bedroom, which was one of the front bedrooms, to the left of the front door as one entered. They took up their posts in the room, and simply sat and listened. The house was very quiet; the other investigators were in their own locations, but everyone was trying to keep noise to a minimum. In order to rule out anyone tainting the data, it was understood that the investigators would try not to talk unless absolutely necessary.

It was just coming to the end of the first half-hour mark, when the team were due to rotate locations. Nothing had happened in Jeanette's room during that time, and the silence from the rest of the team suggested nothing strange had happened to them either. Steve got up and walked to the doorway of Jeanette's room, getting ready to leave.

"All of a sudden," Steve says, "I heard a voice which came from just over my shoulder. It was actually Alicia's voice. And she said, very clearly, 'Are you all right, Stevie?'"

Steve goes on to say, "Now, I don't get called Stevie; it's not a name anyone calls me. But it was Alicia's voice, so I naturally assumed it was her, talking behind me." He turned around. "What?" he said.

Alicia looked at him, startled. "What?"

"What struck me right away," Steve says, "was that when I heard the voice it was right at my shoulder, as if she'd been right behind me. But when I turned around, she wasn't. She was still sitting on the far side of the room, on the other end of the bed. And yet the sound was right there, spoken just into my right ear. I was confused."

"What did you say?" Steve asked her.

"I didn't say anything," Alicia answered.

"Did you not just say 'Stevie?'"

"Stevie?!?"

"I just heard, 'Are you all right, Stevie.' And it was in your voice."

"I didn't say anything. I didn't hear anything, either," Alicia insisted.

"I thought, okay, that's a bit unusual," Steve says, "but I didn't make a note of it, because I thought, I'm dealing with a subjective experience here. It would have been great if someone else had heard it, but they didn't." It did occur to him, however, that if in fact it hadn't been Alicia speaking, then this poltergeist, or whatever it was, had the ability to mimic voices, and that it knew his name, or at least a form of it that he had, thus far, never been addressed as.

The team began rotating their positions, and Steve told the others what he had heard. Alicia repeated her assertion that she had neither spoken nor heard the voice. The occurrence was chalked up to an unknown, and the investigators proceeded with their routine. Steve and Valerie went into the lounge, while Carole went into Jeanette's room alone. Peter and Alicia headed into Jim and Vera's bedroom.

Steve and Valerie had only been sitting in the lounge for a few minutes when they suddenly heard talking. "It was an electronic voice, like someone talking over a radio. But not a radio like a radio station, more like a walkie-talkie or something like that," Steve says.

Carole shouted from Jeanette's bedroom. "Did anybody hear that?"

The entire team had. Everyone converged on Jeanette's room, where Carole was sitting on the bed, pointing at the nightstand beside her. "The clock radio came on," she said.

Steve picked up the radio. It wasn't plugged into the wall, that much was obvious. He turned it over and popped off the backing. There were no batteries in the radio, either. Steve made a quick scan of the area, to see if there were any other devices from which the sound could have come. He saw nothing.

"What did you hear?" he asked. "I heard words, but I couldn't quite make it out."

Carole was adamant that a man's voice had emitted from the powerless clock radio. She was obviously in shock, as she had never experienced anything like this before. The voice, she said, had spoken two clear words: "John's watching."

※

Carole, still flustered, made a note of the words, the location, and the time at which she'd heard the voice: 10:38pm. When asked to clarify, she said the voice had sounded simply like a man speaking over a radio, as if from a taxi. "We know that you can get feedback from various devices, like baby monitors and such, that can pick up taxi radio signals," Steve says. "But the clock radio had no batteries, and wasn't plugged in." The incident was noted as an anomaly, and the investigation continued.

Half an hour passed. During the next rotation, Steve found himself, along with Carole and Valerie, in the unused rear bedroom, the one where Vera's husband had passed away. There were no lamps in this room, so the group were sitting in the dark. Steve sat on the edge of the bed, with Carole on his right and Valerie on his left. They sat there in the blackness, listening. Because of the previous auditory incidents, naturally, their hearing was attuned to the slightest sound, though they were careful to filter out any of the creaks and groans that occur in any normal house.

They sat there for about fifteen minutes without hearing anything out of the ordinary. But then, they heard something strange.

"All of a sudden, from about three or four feet behind me, I heard a rasping breath," Steve says. It was a definite, deliberate sound, as of a man struggling or gasping for air. "What was that?" Steve thought. A few seconds later, the sound came again: a heavy rasp of breath, indisputably human.

He glanced to his left and then his right. Even though the room was quite dark, he could still see the clear outlines of his team members' faces. He could immediately tell from their expressions that they had heard it too. No one moved. Steve wondered if the sound was some sort of residual echo of Vera's dead husband, or if it was simply some auditory trick that wasn't paranormal at all. Slowly, he began to turn his head to peer into the darkness behind him from where the sound had come.

He never got to fully turn around. "I don't recall exactly what happened next," he says, "but the next thing I know, I'm off the bed."

He had, in fact, apparently been propelled off the bed and across the room, suddenly finding himself pressed against the front of the dressing table several feet in front of them. "I literally had to push myself off the table," he says. "I don't know how it happened. One minute I'm over here and then next minute, BANG, I'm over there."

"Oh my God!" said Valerie, and lunged for the wall where she thought a light switch was. Steve had bolted from the room before she even got there, consumed by pain in his back and an intense panic.

He tore into the lounge, which was the first room he saw that had lights on. Peter and Alicia jumped up off the sofa. "What's wrong?" said Peter.

"I've been hit," Steve said, holding his back.

"Let me have a look," Peter said.

Steve lifted his t-shirt, and Peter and Alicia gathered around. There was a large red mark on Steve's back, and a bruise was already beginning to form. Peter began taking photos, asking Steve to describe exactly what had happened. Steve, still panicked, kept repeating, "I don't know. I don't know. One minute I was on the bed, and the next minute I was across the room." It occurred to him, distantly, that he should probably get back to his post in the back bedroom and try to work out exactly what was going on, but at the time, this was the last thing he wanted to do. "I just wanted to leave, to get out of the house," he said. Peter and Alicia were still attempting to question him, but he was in no state to answer them. Instead, he went to the front door, fumbled with the lock, and went outside, where he walked to the end of the driveway and sat on the dividing wall, trying to calm down.

He sat there for nearly twenty minutes, thoughts racing through his head. He wanted very badly to leave and never come back, to discontinue the investigation. But how would he tell the others that he no longer wanted to be involved? He had been doing paranormal investigations for many years at that point, but he had never experienced anything like what had just happened, and he wasn't sure he ever wanted to experience it again.

Peter and Alicia came outside to ask if he was all right. He wasn't, not really, but he didn't tell them that he was considering throwing in the towel. He finally persuaded himself to go back inside the house, but he was, as he put it, "very, very reluctant."

"I was very cautious and very anxious going back in there," he says. "I felt like I was being watched. I felt like I was being *targeted*, actually. The other investigators didn't seem to feel the way I felt, because they hadn't experienced the same thing. I felt like I was being picked on, or something was taking a shot at me. So I gingerly carried on with the investigation."

Once inside, he made himself some tea and toast to calm himself further, and was finally able to articulate to the team what the experience had felt like.

"I'm a big guy," he says, "and it takes a lot to move me four feet across a room. It did have the feeling of a physical punch in the back. It was a hard punch, like a full swing. But at the same time, it was like an electrical shock, like I couldn't stop myself from moving, as though I was repelled. It was a combination of the two things."

Carole and Valerie, for their part, were just as mystified at what had transpired. It had been dark in the room, so they couldn't be entirely certain what had happened, but they both said that Steve had simply been on the bed one second, and across the room the next.

Shaken, the team decided to continue with the rotations. It was half past two in the morning, and one of the team put on the kettle for coffee. It was proving to be a very long night.

CHAPTER FIVE

Steve was heading for the kitchen to pour himself a cup of coffee. Alicia was right behind him. As they crossed the lounge, Steve suddenly stopped dead.

For there, in the middle of the floor of the lounge, was a small statuette of the Greek goddess Themis, commonly known as "Justice." It was a plastic statue, about six inches high, and it certainly had not been there before, on any of their comings and goings through the lounge over the night. If it had been, it would definitely have been noticed or kicked over, because it was standing right in the center of the most common path of travel through the room.

"Where's that come from?" Alicia asked.

Steve bent and picked it up. "I don't know. I've never seen it before." He called in the rest of the team, and asked if anyone else had noticed it, or seen where it had come from. No one had. Peter wondered if perhaps it had been knocked over when they had been setting up equipment, but its upright position and sudden appearance several hours after their arrival made that scenario unlikely. It seemed as though it had been placed there deliberately, as if someone or something had wanted to make sure no one could miss it.

Steve put it on the fireplace mantel for the moment, and the team talked among themselves. They decided that they should watch the 360-degree videoscope they had taken of the house when they first arrived, to see where the object had been at the outset. The investigators rewound the video and forwarded through it, searching every room for the statuette. Despite their close scrutiny, they couldn't see it on the tape anywhere. So where had it come from? They made a note to ask Jim and Vera where the statue was usually kept, and chalked it up to yet another mystery in a night that was so far brimming with them.

※

A short time later, as the team were still standing in the lounge marveling about the apparent movement of the Themis statue, Alicia suddenly let out a gasp. She had been standing near the door into the kitchen, and when everyone turned to look, they immediately saw what she had gasped at.

The surface of the door had instantly become studded with countless beads of water, which then began to drip slowly towards the floor. "I noticed the bottom of the door was wet and was about to alert the others when thousands of tiny droplets instantaneously covered the entire door. It happened right before my eyes," she said.

"The water appeared in the blink of an eye, just in a flash," Steve says. "It wasn't there and then it just was." He notes that the water simply seemed to have appeared there in bead form, not as if had seeped out of the door or been thrown or flicked there; the droplets were perfectly formed and round, not spattered. He felt around to the back of the door, the side that faced the kitchen, and it was bone dry. The water dripped down the door for about two minutes, after which it simply dried up, very quickly, just as it had on the ceiling on their previous visit. After a minute or two, the side of the door facing the lounge was likewise dry to the touch.

Steve, fascinated by this new iteration of the water phenomena, kept expecting a return of the more dramatic water manifestations they'd witnessed before, like the downpour in the kitchen or the intelligently moving tendrils on the hallway ceiling. His camera was at the ready. But apparently the water on the door was the only such incident of that type they would see that time around.

After a while, they gave up watching for more of that strange rainfall, and simply began talking among themselves again, preparing to pack up their equipment, and making notes about everything they had witnessed during the course of the night. It was sunrise, and they were all simply wandering around, and thinking of making some breakfast before the Gardners were due to return.

Suddenly, Valerie, who was in the hallway with Carole, called out. "Steve! Come here a minute."

Steve went into the hallway. There he found Valerie, Carole, and Alicia, who had come out from one of the other rooms. They were all standing there, sniffing the air.

As Steve approached them, he was hit by a very strong, distinctive fragrance.

"Can you smell that?" Valerie asked.

He could. "It smells like flowers," he said. The aroma was potent, as though the flowers were right under his nose.

Peter came into the hallway. Steve asked, "Can you smell anything?"

Peter nodded. "Flowers. Really strong," he said.

The smell persisted for quite a while, not fading in all of that time. Steve notes that there were no flowers present in the house, and indeed that the entire house smelled of nothing so much as damp, like a wet dog. The floral scent was strongest right beneath the spot where they'd seen the water snaking across the ceiling. After about ten minutes, the smell was gone as suddenly as it had appeared. Steve also noted that when he read the reports of the individual investigators later, he saw that three of them had mentioned another very strong smell, of tobacco with a distinct hint of licorice. While this smell had only lasted from twenty to forty seconds in those cases, the three investigators who reported it had noticed it in three different locations in the house, when the team had been separated.

Afterwards, breakfast was made and eaten, and equipment was packed away. There was nothing to do now but wait for the family to return home. Jim and Vera arrived a little early, at about 9:45am. Jeanette was not with them; she had chosen to stay at her aunt's house for one more day.

The first thing out of Vera's mouth when she entered the house was, "So, how was your night?"

※

Steve asked the Gardners to come into the lounge so that the team could give them a rundown of what they had experienced. He wanted to tone down the incidents somewhat, to avoid upsetting the family further, but the small smirk on Jim's face as he settled into his chair in the lounge suggested he knew what the team was up to. His expression seemed to say, "Well, lay it on me."

Steve went over and picked up the Themis statuette from the mantel, showing it to Vera. "First question," he said. "Is this yours?"

Vera said that it was.

"It's Themis, isn't it?"

"Yeah," Vera said. "We picked that up when we were on holiday."

"Where was this statue?" Steve asked.

"It was next to the television. Just on the right side of the telly," Vera answered. She pointed to a spot on the TV stand. There was a small vase on the left side of the television, but the right side was obviously empty.

"How long have you had this?"

"God, I've had that for years. John bought it for me."

Steve hesitated. He remembered the voice that Carole had heard coming out of the clock radio, the one that had said, "John's watching." Steve looked at Vera. "Who's John?" he asked.

Vera tilted her head. "Well, my husband. You know, the one who died."

"His name's John?" Steve said, incredulous.

"Yes."

"When did he buy you this?"

Vera thought back. "We went on holiday…must

have been about fifteen years ago. We just got it in one of those little gift shops, as a souvenir to take home."

"Why Themis?" Steve wanted to know.

"No particular reason," Vera said, clearly wondering what the point of all this was. "We just liked it."

Steve asked if the statuette had always been there on the right side of the television, and Vera said it had been there since she'd gotten it. Steve then explained to the Gardners that the team had taken a 360-degree video of the lounge a mere twenty-five minutes after Jim and Vera had left the previous day. He brought out the tape and rewound it so that the Gardners could watch.

As the video panned slowly around the room, the vase on the left of the television came into view, exactly where it was supposed to be. Of course, Vera and Jim were expecting to see the Themis statue at the right of the TV, just where it had always been, but on the video, it wasn't there. Vera was puzzled. "But it's always there!" she insisted, noting the time stamp on the video. "Where's it gone? How come it's not on there? When did it move?"

Steve told them he had no idea when the object had seemingly disappeared from its usual place; he only knew that it hadn't been there when they had taken the video, and hadn't appeared until roughly seven hours later, when it had inexplicably turned up right in the middle of the lounge floor. Where had it been all that time? "We would have noticed straight away if something had been moved, if it had been on the tape," Steve says. He points out that for all he knew, the object could have disappeared while the Gardners were still in the house, and they just hadn't noticed its absence. In the interest of thoroughness, Steve measured the distance between where Vera said the object had been originally and the spot where it reappeared. The distance was 58.2 inches. Steve noted this in his report.

Steve then wanted to concentrate on John. No one on the team had known Vera's dead husband was named John; the name had never come up. "How did John die?" Steve asked.

Vera said, "He had a heart attack. He died in the back bedroom. Died in bed, actually."

Then Steve asked, "What brought on the heart attack?"

"Oh, he had a lot of health problems," Vera answered. "Emphysema. He was always struggling for breath."

The investigators traded glances, but didn't tell Vera that they'd heard rasping breaths several times during the night. Steve continued his questioning. "Did he work?"

"Oh yeah," Vera said. "He was a taxi driver."

A silence fell over the room. Carole approached Steve and asked if she could have a word with him. Steve excused himself and followed Carole into the kitchen. "Do you think what I heard could have been a taxi radio transmission?" Carole whispered.

"Possible, I suppose," Steve said. It certainly did seem as though the phenomena were being caused by the spirit of Vera's dead husband, but Steve had seen other cases of poltergeist phenomena in which the entity, or whatever it was, could mimic the trappings of a haunting, especially if the family experiencing the incidents believed they were caused by a ghost. He thought that might be the case here, especially since Vera had specifically told him early on in the investigation that she thought John might be haunting her. Perhaps the family were "creating" a spirit because that's what they expected. "There was really no reason for a haunting to begin so suddenly," Steve says. "It had just started out of the blue, ten months earlier. John had been dead for quite a long time at this point, and Vera and Jim had been married for more than two years. It didn't make sense that a spirit was suddenly upset about her remarriage, such a long time after the fact."

Steve and Carole returned to the lounge. Now Steve was curious about Jeanette, since he suspected she may be the focus of the activity, and he was still wondering if she was the one causing it, even though she had not been present. He asked Vera how Jeanette had acted at her aunt's house.

"She didn't have a very restful night, actually," Vera answered. "She was agitated, and couldn't sleep. She was up and down all night. She just never seemed comfortable there. On edge the whole time."

Steve nodded, thinking that perhaps his hunch had been right, and that they were dealing with a very rare translocational focus, who could affect things from a distance. After he had noted this information, he simply gave Vera and Jim a broad summary of the incidents they'd experienced in the night, keeping it relatively non-committal. They had heard some sounds, he said, and smelled some unusual odors. He told them about the water that had appeared on the door. He didn't say anything out loud, but he was excited about the phenomena the team had experienced during the night, and was eager to set up yet another investigation, with the family in the home this time, for comparison. The Gardners were amenable to this, so the team said they'd be in touch, and left.

CHAPTER SIX

Later that day, after some much-needed sleep, Steve and the team began reviewing the notes, photos and video they'd taken during their stay. They had watched the videoscope a couple of times before, briefly scanning through it to see where the statuette had come from, but this time they sat down and watched it more intently. And it was then that they noticed something rather astonishing.

The main video camera, of course, had been set up in the corner of the lounge facing the TV, taking in the whole room. At one point in the video, Steve says, "We saw something like smoke, that seemed to come out from the television screen, go up above the television, and then shoot back into the television screen again. You can clearly see it. At first you think it's a reflection in the screen, but then it comes above the television into the air, and back into the TV again. It was very close in location to where the statuette should have been. We were excited we'd caught that on video."

The team didn't hear from Vera for the week before the second investigation took place. When the day arrived, the same five investigators sat with the Gardners again and asked if anything had happened in the interim. The couple described several similar incidents as before, including a couple of the water manifestations. They said on one occasion, water had formed on the ceiling over their bed in the middle of the night. They woke up at ten past two in the morning, with rain falling heavily upon them. Understandably, this caused some panic, as they were trying to get out of bed and stumbling around in the dark for the light switch and plastic sheeting to protect the bedding. This rain lasted five or six minutes.

They also saw things fly off the windowsill while Vera was doing the dishes; specifically, a plant and a couple of ornaments came flying at her while she was standing at the sink. There had also been further auditory disturbances: footsteps, coughing, and the like. Steve asked Vera if she still thought the sounds were associated with her dead husband. She looked at him oddly and said, "Actually, I do, yeah." Steve told her he didn't want to go into anything at that time, as they were still analyzing the information they had and were waiting until the end of the investigation to sort everything out and try to come to some conclusion.

The Gardners said that the council had also visited again during the week, and had left another incident report form. It was held on the refrigerator with a magnet, and Steve noticed that several of the new incidents they had described were written there. Vera said the man from the council had only asked them a few questions and left the new form there while taking the other one away to put in the file that was being kept on the Gardner home.

After their talk, Steve and the team began to set up their equipment again. The plan was to stay for seven hours, as they had on the previous occasion. They arrived in the morning, and hoped to stay all day, since they'd already done an overnight investigation. Steve told the family that he wanted them to simply act as they would if the team was not there, and go about things as they normally would during the day. He didn't want to alter the environment more than necessary, so he told the family to ignore the team as much as possible so that he could monitor them in their home without being too intrusive.

Jeanette was present, but Steve noticed that she tended to keep to herself. She didn't speak to the team to any great degree, but still seemed interested in what was going on, periodically coming out of her bedroom to listen to them talking.

When everything was squared away, Steve went into the back bedroom. "It was a whole different room in the daylight," he says, chuckling. The other members of the team dispersed to other parts of the house. For the first few hours, absolutely nothing unusual happened at all. There were no strange noises, no significant temperature changes, no object movement, no water formation. When lunchtime rolled around, the team took a break to eat and have another chat with Vera. She didn't discuss their particular case at that time, but simply made small talk, asking Steve how long he had been a parapsychologist. Steve answered her questions, trying to keep everything as calm and normal as possible.

After lunch, the team decided to expand their investigation to the outside of the house, in particular the garden area. Armed with handheld geomagnetic and electromagnetic meters, along with several other devices, they scanned the area around the home, searching for any anomalies. Nothing unusual was noted, so the team made their way back inside.

Steve asked Vera how often incidents happened during the day. She told him that while the phenomena were more frequent at night, things often did happen during the day, but that the events always came out of the blue. She hadn't noticed any particular pattern to the times of the occurrences, and said that they could happen anytime, often when they least expected it.

At about ten past four, as the team were gathered in the lounge, the curtains on the front window moved of their own accord. No windows were open, though the weather outside was still quite hot. As the team watched, the curtain bellowed out and inwards, just as if there had been a breeze, but there was no breeze or draft that anyone could feel. It happened once, and then the curtain settled back as though nothing had happened. All of the team still had their devices on and working, but none of them registered anything untoward. The ambiguous movement of the curtain was, oddly, the only incident that occurred on the second investigation.

At the end of the day, the team packed up their equipment, slightly disappointed that this stage of the operation had yielded so little. The investigation was still far from over, though; they still had to compile all their notes, contact the council, study lab reports, and try to put together some plan of action for the family. As Steve and the others were leaving, Vera asked, "Are you going to be able to help us?"

Steve asked, "Well, what do you actually want? What do you want us to do?"

Vera broke down crying. "I've lived here for fourteen years," she said. "I love this place. I don't really want to move." Utmost in her mind, of course, was the fact that the house held memories of her dead husband that she was reluctant to leave behind.

"Well, if there's something we can do, we will,"

Steve assured her. "But out of curiosity, if the council was to offer a new place, what would you do?"

Vera clearly didn't know what to say, so Jim jumped in. "We'll have a talk about that," he said.

Steve didn't push the issue. He just told them to talk about what they wanted to do if the phenomena didn't stop. Obviously, he had to take into consideration the fact that he was not only dealing with the residents of the property, but also the council, who owned the home. The council had made it clear that they were very keen not to let further publicity about the case get out, in case they needed to rent the property to someone else at some stage.

The team told the Gardners they would be back in touch in a few days, and left to put their equipment back into their cars. At this point, Steve was curious to speak to the priest at the church near the house, as he knew that the man had heard of the disturbances and might have some further insights about the family. Steve had actually never spoken to the priest in person, though he had chatted with him briefly on the phone, and he thought now was as good a time as any. So while the rest of the team headed back to headquarters, Steve and Peter walked around the corner to the church.

CHAPTER SEVEN

The steeple of Saint John the Baptist Catholic Church was visible over the rooftops of Foxholes Close, and in fact the church itself lay directly behind the Gardners' property. It served not only as a place of comfort for Vera in particular, but also as a means of employment: the septuagenarian worked there as a cleaner part time, and had a good relationship with the priest, Rev. Michael Jones. The newspaper article that had first piqued Steve's interest in the case had mentioned that Rev. Jones had performed a blessing on the home, which had apparently done nothing to assuage the phenomena.

Steve and Peter entered Saint John's and saw the priest right away, and identified themselves. The priest invited them into the back of the church so that they could talk in his office. Rev. Jones seemed a friendly and no-nonsense man, and was quite happy to tell them everything he knew about the case.

Once they were all seated, the priest asked, "How have things been for Jim and Vera?"

"Well, it's obviously been traumatizing for them," Steve said. "They've certainly been having some difficulty, especially considering the damage to the inside of the home. Vera told me that you'd visited the location. What do you think is going on?"

Rev. Jones confirmed that he'd been to the property to perform a blessing, which he regretted had not seemed to help. And then, to Steve's surprise, he stated baldly, "They've got a poltergeist."

"I was quite taken aback, actually, because this was a Catholic Church," Steve says. "It's very rare that a Catholic priest would be this forward regarding the paranormal. But he seemed familiar with the concept of poltergeists, and seemed to know something about parapsychological theories surrounding them. I hadn't expected that."

Another thing that Steve didn't expect was that Rev. Jones had actually witnessed phenomena in the Gardner home with his own eyes. On one visit, he claimed, he'd been sitting with Vera in the lounge when a large painting of a tiger that had been hanging over the fireplace—a framed foil rendering of the type popular in Britain in the 1980s, measuring about two feet wide—suddenly flew off the wall, sailed across the room, and hit him on the side of the leg.

Rev. Jones further stated that out of concern for the family, and after his initial blessing had been ineffective, he had contacted the head diocese to ask about possibly performing an exorcism at the Foxholes Close property. However, after hearing the priest's case, the diocese had determined that the phenomena was likely poltergeist-related, and therefore didn't warrant church intervention. The justification they used, Rev. Jones said, was that since poltergeist phenomena, after fakery had been ruled out, are generally accepted to be person-based rather than location-based, and do not involve anything like demonic possession, then the intervention of an exorcist would not alleviate the disturbances, and may in fact make them worse. The priest accepted this, and simply continued to be supportive for Vera and the Gardners, which was all he could reasonably do at that point.

"You are aware that Vera's former husband died in the house?" Steve asked.

Rev. Jones was aware, but stated that he didn't think the phenomena was related to John's death. After all, he said, Vera had never had problems in the house until recently, and John had been dead for many years. Steve had been thinking along similar lines, of course, and said as much.

Steve then asked Rev. Jones if he thought Jeanette was the focus, and the priest said he couldn't really say for sure. But then he added an interesting piece of information. "Jim and Vera have had quite a few problems with Jeanette, you know," he said.

"Oh, really? I didn't know," Steve said. "What sorts of problems?"

"Well, she got herself pregnant," Rev. Jones answered.

"Did she?" None of this had come up in any of their conversations with the Gardners, and Steve was intrigued.

"Oh yes. She's got a child," Rev. Jones said. "A daughter. But she doesn't live with her."

"Where's the daughter now?" Steve asked.

"She lives with a foster family, because Jeanette couldn't really look after her."

Steve was still reeling from this revelation. Could this be further evidence of Jeanette's role in causing the disturbances? The stress caused by having a child taken away must have been enormous, and could have unsettled the family dynamic to such a degree that paranormal phenomena resulted. "Does the family see the daughter?" he asked.

"Yes, she's been to the house a few times. Someone from the foster family brought her."

"Has anything happened in the house while Jeanette's daughter was there?" Steve asked.

The priest answered immediately. "Oh yes. On one occasion, when Jeanette had the daughter staying in her bedroom, all hell broke loose in there."

"What do you mean, 'all hell broke loose'?" Steve asked.

"Just things being thrown all over the place, objects flying around," Rev. Jones said. "The little girl was apparently hit with a hair dryer that flew off the dresser. She screamed and ran out of the bedroom, along with Jeanette. The daughter wouldn't come to the house after that."

"What's the present situation, then?" Steve wanted to know.

"Well, now Jeanette goes to visit the girl at the foster home. She has visitation every two weeks or so."

It seemed that the case for Jeanette being the focus was growing ever stronger, and the priest must have instinctively known that Steve was thinking this, because he added, "The family have been through some rough financial times, too, of course. That was why I offered Vera the part-time job here, to help them out with money."

Steve had to admit he hadn't really been aware of the extent to which the priest had been involved in the family's life, and felt somewhat conflicted that so many of the family's difficulties had been kept from the team. The financial and emotional turmoil the Gardners had been experiencing was obviously relevant to the case, and he was glad that at least Rev. Jones had opened up to them and clarified the family's situation. It would help them to develop a clearer picture of the disturbances, and hopefully help both the family and the council achieve the outcome that would be best for everyone.

Before leaving, Steve and Peter gave Rev. Jones a brief summary of what they had found in their investigation. They didn't go into much detail, but they thought the man had a right to know what had been going on, especially after he had helped the Gardners so much. They then told him that the team still had to have a meeting with the council to decide a plan of action, and that he would of course be informed about what developed, either from them or from Vera herself. Then, their minds racing with all of this new data, they headed back to MAPIT to reconvene with the rest of the team.

CHAPTER EIGHT

Two days later, Peter Hough got a call from Northwest Laboratories, who had finished their analysis of the water samples that the team had sent several weeks before.

Lab tech Kevin Platt told Peter that a hard copy of the analysis would be arriving soon in the mail, but that he would give a rundown over the phone. "Now, where did these samples come from again?"

"Just where we told you," Peter said. "One was a control sample from a bathroom tap from a home in Foxholes Close, Rochdale. The other came from a ceiling in the same home. That was the suspect sample, the one that was behaving unusually," Peter answered.

"All right. Just verifying our information," Kevin said. "Let's start with Sample B, which was the control sample. This was completely ordinary tap water. No fluoridation, but that's standard for the area. The UCSMs read 93."

"What are UCSMs?" Peter asked.

Kevin explained that UCSMs were simply a measurement of the very small electrical charge that water picks up when it is run through copper pipes. In low quantities, he said, this electrical charge is completely harmless, and the water is perfectly safe to drink. "The normal range of UCSMs in tap water," he said, "is 70 to 108. So this fell right into the middle. There were also no unusual chemicals in the sample, or anything of that sort. As I said, totally ordinary."

Peter could sense that Kevin was building suspense, so he asked, "And what about the suspect sample?"

"Well, that's quite a different story," Kevin said. "There were some different chemical amounts in the ceiling sample that weren't in the tap sample, though that isn't really what's unusual. If this water was obtained from the ceiling, then we would expect to see things like higher concentrations of paint chemicals, gypsum, and the like. The chemicals would leach in from the surface they were sitting on, which in this case was a ceiling. Per our analysis of the materials on a similar type of ceiling, the chemical makeup of the water was about what you would expect it to be, considering where it was gathered from."

"Well, what else is unusual?" Peter asked. "Is there another difference between the tap water and the suspect water?"

"Oh yeah," Kevin said. "There's a massive difference."

At this point, Peter felt the need to clarify, "This was the water that was behaving strangely. It was moving intelligently across the ceiling."

"Well, I can't speak to that," Kevin said. "But what I can tell you is that the UCSMs are off the charts."

Peter's heart began to thump. "Meaning…?"

"The UCSMs on the ceiling sample were well over 1,000. 1,323, to be precise."

"How can that be?" Peter asked. "How can there be that much electricity in the water?" He almost couldn't believe what he was hearing.

"That's the thing. We don't know," Kevin said. "It's electrically driven."

"But how could you get that?"

Kevin chuckled. "Well, you don't get it out of the tap, that's for sure. It definitely isn't tap water."

"Well, where's it coming from?" Peter asked.

"We have no idea. We just don't see that sort of thing. It's as if the water is electrically induced somehow."

Peter racked his brain to try to think of some rational explanation for these astounding results. "Would it be easy to manufacture something like that?" he said.

"Not impossible, but not easy," Kevin answered. "Water and electricity don't mix very well, as you can imagine." He laughed. "But it's really unusual. We almost never see UCSMs that high. I don't really know what else to tell you. We're as confused as you are."

Peter rang off, more excited than he'd been in weeks. Here was the leading water analysis lab in the United Kingdom telling him that the water they had seen snaking its way across a ceiling was pulsing with electricity to an almost impossible degree. Even if it didn't definitively prove that the water manifestations were paranormal, the lab analysis would surely be enough to prove to the council that the Gardners hadn't simply been throwing tap water around their house. And if the council could be convinced that the family hadn't been faking that phenomena, maybe they could be convinced that the rest of the disturbances were genuine too. All that was left to do was compile all the data, and go to see the council.

☙❧

Two days after the MAPIT report on the property at Foxholes Close was completed, Steve and his four investigators were sitting in a boardroom across from five members of the Rochdale Council.

Steve was amused, since only two council members had been present for their first meeting; obviously the Gardner case was causing some curiosity in the council offices.

The team opened their files and began laying out their findings. "We understand the difficult situation the council are in," Steve said. "You have tenants who are having a hard time living in the environment, and as the owners you have an obligation to make the environment livable for your clients. We hope everyone can come to a reasonable solution."

The council members agreed that they hoped the situation could be resolved to the satisfaction of all parties.

"From the information we gathered from our investigations," Steve announced, "we believe that they are having some type of paranormal disturbances there."

The council members exchanged glances and smirks. One of them spoke up. "You mean it's actually happening?"

"Yes," Steve said. "We've witnessed it ourselves."

The smirks turned to expressions of shock. "You all saw it?" the council member said.

"Yes. We also got photos of it." Enjoying their discomfort somewhat, Steve passed around the photos they'd taken at the Gardner home. The council members peered at the photos, shaking their heads and looking nervously at one another.

"This is definitely *not* the family throwing water around," Steve said.

One of the council members looked up from a photo. "But how do you know?"

"The family weren't there. We sent them away. We eliminated that possibility." He pointed to a photo of the water beaded on the lounge door. "That happened when the family were not present." He also told them about the results from the water analysis, and made it clear to them that the water they had witnessed behaving unusually had most assuredly not come from the city's water supply.

To a man, the council members seemed befuddled. Steve was slightly taken aback by this. "Their reaction suggested that they had been expecting us to come in and tell them it was all a hoax," he says. "It seems they hadn't really thought about what they were going to do if it wasn't. They didn't have a secondary protocol planned in case it was real. That surprised me quite a bit."

Steve made his concerns very clear to them. "Guys," he said, "what are you going to do? Did you not even consider that this might really be happening?"

No one seemed to want to admit that they had not considered it, but they quickly began making noises that, of course, something would be done to help the family as quickly as possible. Steve suggested that they consult with the family to work out what was to be done; as both the Gardners and the council were his clients, it was not his place to interfere with any decisions to be made. He had simply conducted the investigation to determine if there had been any fakery present, and since he had found none, further actions would be left in the hands of the council and their tenants.

※

Several days later, Steve called Vera and asked if the council had been in touch with her. She said that two of them had come to the house, one of them a housing officer. The council had told the Gardners that they would be quite happy to relocate them.

"In fact, they're giving us a bigger place," Vera said. She didn't sound terribly enthused.

"Is that what you want?," Steve asked. "Because you told me you didn't want to move."

"I don't, really," Vera said. "But everything's getting ruined. We can't live like this."

"Are you sure about this?" Steve asked. Vera said that she was, and added that she was due to have a meeting with the council in four days' time to finalize the details. Steve told her to keep him apprised of the situation, and rang off.

He then called the council himself. They confirmed that they had been to visit the Gardners and that the Gardners had agreed to be relocated to a four-bedroom house about a mile and a half away. They also noted that the family didn't really warrant a four-bedroom home, since there were only three of them, but the council was clearly trying to sweeten the deal to avoid more publicity about the disturbances. So far, the only information that had gone public about the case was the initial newspaper article, and the council were eager to keep it that way. Steve thanked them, and said the team would keep in touch.

Next, Steve visited the Rev. Jones again, and found him just as friendly and receptive as before. The priest was happy at the news of the family's relocation, and expressed a wish that the Gardners would be able to get some peace in their new home.

"I just hope it doesn't follow them," Rev. Jones said. "That happens a lot of times, doesn't it?"

Steve was again struck by how much the priest seemed to know about poltergeist phenomena. "Sometimes, yes," Steve said.

"Well, maybe if they're in a different environment that they feel better about, everything will stop," Rev. Jones said. He seemed to understand that even though classic poltergeist infestations are person-based, the environment the people found themselves in could also have a significant effect. He told Steve that Vera was going to continue working at the church, and that she would be able to keep him updated on any further happenings. Steve was satisfied with that, and bid the priest goodbye.

The original newspaper article from the *Manchester Evening News* that sparked Steve's interest.

Two shots of the exterior of the house at Foxholes Close in 1995.

The church behind the house, where Mrs. Gardner worked as a cleaner.

The house interior, hallway and kitchen.

An example of the water damage evident on the ceiling.

Mysterious beads of water that appeared spontaneously on the door of the lounge.

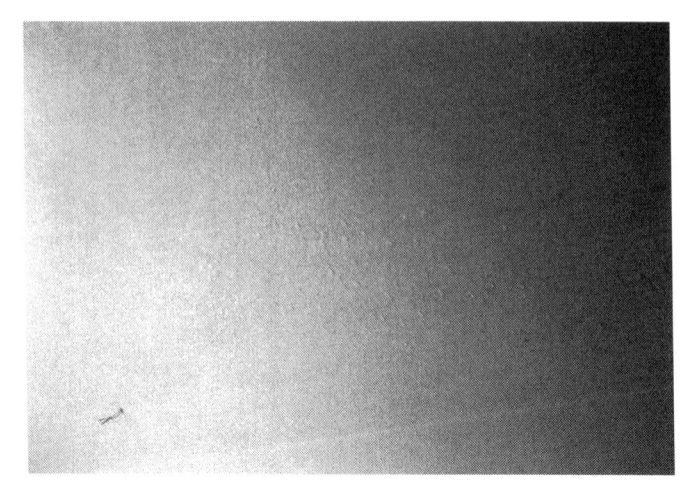

Steve Mera noting the movement of a tendril of water around a light fixture.

Alicia during the second investigation.

Closer views of the water that appeared on the hallway ceiling and snaked around the fixture. Lab analysis of the water showed that it was intensely electrically charged.

The traveling Themis statue.

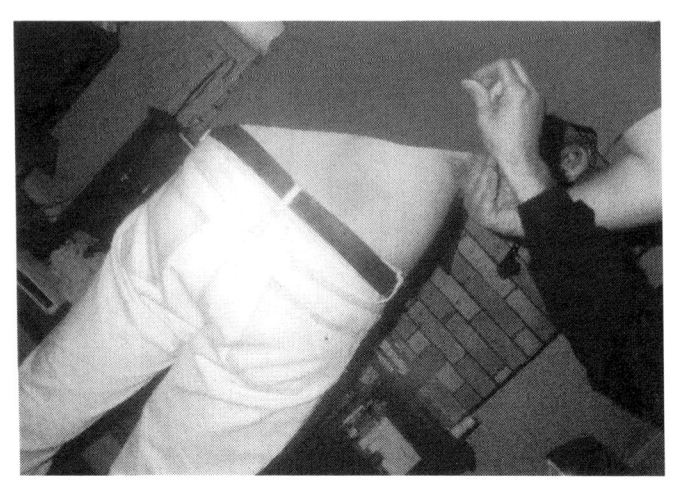

The red mark that appeared on Steve's back after he was hit by an unseen force in the back bedroom.

The team dig in the back garden after a strange tip from a psychic.

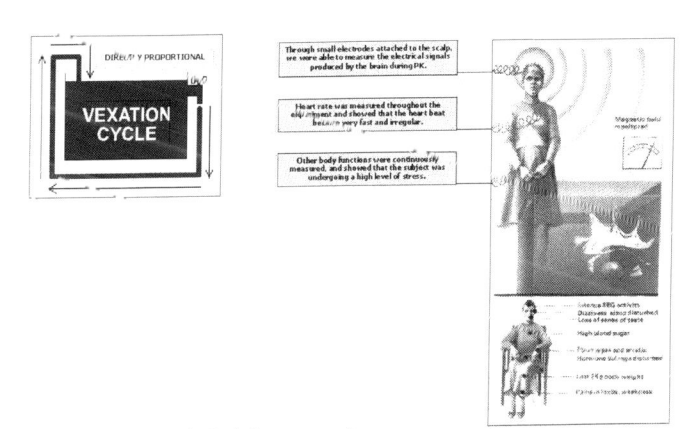

Drawings and field notes done during the investigation.

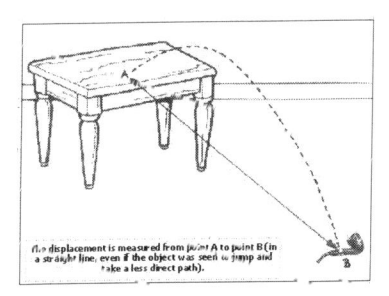

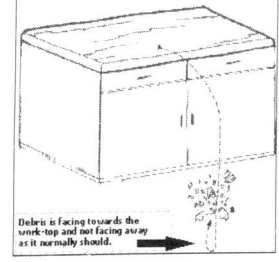

North West Water

North West Water Limited
Lingley Mere Laboratory
PO Box 458
Warrington
WA5 3QT
Telephone: 01925 783000
Direct line:
Facsimile:

Your ref
Our ref   19/09/96
Date

Dear Sir,

With reference to the two samples you sent in for analysis, I have pleasure in enclosing the results of the limited tests we have been able to carry out on the small amount of suspect sample.

Whilst the results for the tap sample are typical for those determinands listed, the suspect sample results are higher except for magnesium. We can only conclude from this that the high results are due to leaching of components from the plaster into the water.

If we can be of any assistance in the future do not hesitate to contact us, however whilst we have been happy to carry out the initial analysis free of charge, any future analysis would incurr our normal commercial costs.

yours sincerely

Kevin Platt
Customer Support Team

Registered in England and Wales. Registered No. 2366678
Registered Office: Dawson House, Great Sankey, Warrington, WA5 3LW

Cover letter of the hard copy of the lab analysis of the ceiling water.

NWW LABORATORY SERVICES
SAMPLE REPORT ON TAP/SUSPECT SAMPLE EX NARO

DETERMINAND	UNITS	SUSPECT SAMPLE	TAP SAMPLE
CALCIUM	MG/L	106	14
MAGNESIUM	MG/L	8	7
SODIUM	MG/L	197	12
CHLORIDE	MG/L	198.43	10.66
CONDUCTIVITY	USCM	1323	181

?

KEVIN PLATT
CUSTOMER SUPPORT TEAM

Lab comparison of the ceiling water sample with the control from the tap. Note significant discrepancy in conductivity.

CHAPTER NINE

A week later, Steve got a phone call from Jim.

"We've been offered this new place," Jim said. "We're due to move into it on Thursday." He said they'd been down to look at the property, and added that the council had even helped them pack their things and were going to provide transportation to the new house. Steve thought that was great news, that the council were so willing to help the family out. It was the least they could do, Steve thought, after giving the Gardners such a rough ride before, when they all but accused the family of faking the phenomena.

A week after that, Steve called Jim and asked how the new house was.

"Oh, it's really nice," he said. "It's big. It's great, we've got loads of room."

"Anything unusual going on there?" Steve asked.

"Well, I haven't noticed anything," Jim answered.

Not really a no, Steve thought. "Are you sure there's been nothing?" he asked. True, the family had only been in the new place for one day at that point, but Steve was still curious.

"Oh, well," Jim said dismissively, "Jeanette said there were a couple of little things, things moving in her bedroom."

Ah, now we're getting to the bottom of it. "What things?" Steve asked.

"She has a sort of wind-up toy in her bedroom," Jim said. "She said it came flying off the shelf and smashed on the floor." He noted that he hadn't seen it himself, but had heard Jeanette talking about it. Steve wondered to himself if this could just be what he calls "teething problems," a brief resurgence of the phenomena in a new environment that would likely fizzle out quickly once everything had settled down. He said as much to Jim.

"Yeah, we'll see," Jim said. "Hopefully everything will be fine." There was a pause. Steve was about to say goodbye, but then Jim said, "Oh, last thing. I just remembered. I've got to tell you this."

"What's that?" Steve asked.

"Well, we left the old house, and then the council went to look over the place after we handed the keys in. They rang me up a day or so later. They were really angry with me."

"Why?" Steve said.

"Well, they were complaining because apparently, I'd left all the windows open," Jim said. "The door was locked, but every single window in the place was left open." His tone turned indignant. "I told them I never left all the windows open. Everything was locked up when we left. I'm not bloody daft. I told them straight, I locked that bloody place up." He was obviously quite put out that the council were still blaming him for things he didn't do, even after the paranormal team had made it clear that the family's complaints had been legitimate. Steve told Jim to keep him posted if the incidents continued, and they could figure out together what could be done.

As part of the follow-up protocol on the case, Steve then contacted the council. He told them about the procedure that MAPIT called "the safety pattern," also known as "fallowing the home." He explained that this was always done where possible, to try to stop phenomena continuing at a location after the residents are gone.

"Basically, what we do is deprive the location of electricity, even from the mains," he says. "We try to do this for a period of at least seven or eight months, if we can. Also, we make it plain that no one should go into the property in that time." The logic behind this, he says, is to try to "starve" the phenomena of energy, both human and electrical. Obviously, he points out, it's not always possible to fallow the home for that long a stretch, but MAPIT considers it an ideal situation, and he notes that it does seem to work in most cases to end the disturbances.

The council were amenable to this proposal, and as it turned out, things went better than expected; the Foxholes Close property was allowed to sit empty for nearly eleven months. No new residents moved in, and the electricity remained off. No one entered the home, and it was kept locked and secured.

After the fallow period had passed, the council decided it was safe to rent it out to someone else, and proceeded to do so, letting the home to a Korean family. After the new family had been in the house for nearly two months, Steve went to pay them a visit. Not wanting to cause any undue suspicion or influence the family's reports, Steve told the woman who answered his knock that he was in the area conducting a survey. He asked if anyone in the home had experienced anything strange.

The woman looked at him blankly. "What do you mean?"

"Just anything unusual," Steve said. He then made up a story that there was a suspected underground gas leak and tremors in the area, and that he was simply doing a routine survey of residents to check if there were any problems. "We're just making sure everything is safe," he assured her.

The woman said that she hadn't experienced anything odd at all, and seemingly had no idea what he could possibly be getting at. Steve thanked her and left, quite happy that the activity at the home seemed to have stopped, at long last.

❦

It wasn't long afterwards, though, that Steve got another call from Jim.

"We've had some things happening again," Jim said.

As soon as he could, Steve gathered two members of his team and went to see the Gardners in the new house. A distraught Vera told them that objects had been flying off shelves and counters again, just as they had at the old place. She didn't report any water manifestations or auditory phenomena, but noted several instances of object movement. In one instance, she said that she and Jeanette had been in the kitchen when a cup had gone flying off the windowsill and onto the floor. Jim had been out at the time, and could not confirm this, but believed his wife's account.

In another instance, Vera said, her clock had come flying off the fireplace in the lounge.

"Where were you when this happened?" Steve asked.

"In the lounge," Vera said.

"And where was Jeanette?"

"She was in the lounge too."

"Was there anything else?" Steve said.

"Well, something happened in Jeanette's bedroom while I was in the kitchen. I heard Jeanette scream and then she ran into the kitchen and said something had flown across the room."

Steve silently noted that Jeanette had been present at every single incident. Acting on a hunch, he asked when Jeanette was going to be out of the house next.

"She's going out on Tuesday at around eleven," Vera said. Steve said he would come back while Jeanette was gone.

Tuesday came, and Steve returned to the house, where he set up a few hidden cameras in strategic locations. A few days later, he came back to retrieve them.

The footage on the cameras confirmed what Steve had suspected: Jeanette had been throwing the objects herself. In one instance, Jeanette had very clearly picked up a small knick-knack off the windowsill while her mother's back was turned, then thrown it forcefully against a wall, all while making an enormous fuss. "Oh no, it's back again!" she shrieked. "It's back for me!" When a startled Vera turned to witness the carnage, Jeanette naturally told her mother that the object had flown across the room of its own accord.

Steve, for his part, was not surprised in the least that Jeanette had resorted to such tactics. She had, after all, spent the previous year as the center of attention, with newspaper articles being written about her family, and investigators trooping in and out of the house. She was obviously missing all the activity, and acted out in the only way she knew how. Steve notes that this is a very common occurrence when poltergeist infestations draw investigation and media attention, particularly when a child—or, in this case, a childlike adult—is involved. Even the famous Enfield case, which was mostly deemed genuine by paranormal investigators at the time, contained a handful of incidents that were obviously faked by the focus, Janet Hodgson.

Jim and Vera, though, were shocked when they watched the video of Jeanette's stunts. Vera wondered aloud to Steve if Jeanette had been responsible for all the disturbances at their old house as well, but Steve assured her that this was impossible. He pointed out that Jeanette had not been present when the investigators witnessed some of the phenomena, like the appearance of the beaded water on the door or the apportation of the statuette. Additionally, he reminded her, there were cameras rolling that would have easily caught her if she had been throwing things, just as easily as they had caught her this time. Finally, Steve said, there would have been no way for

Jeanette to have faked the water manifestations at all, not only because the investigators had seen and photographed the water moving intelligently on its own, but also because the water had been analyzed and had definitely not come from the home's water supply.

Vera and Jim were satisfied with this, and the team took their leave, with at least one mystery solved. When the Gardners later confronted Jeanette, she confessed to throwing the objects, and the family then settled back into a normalcy that had been a long time coming.

❦

Meanwhile, Steve discovered that the Korean family who had moved into the Foxholes Close home had moved out after only six months. Steve contacted the council, curious as to the reason. The council told him that the family had simply decided to move to a different area, and hadn't reported anything wrong with the home that was causing them to move. They also told him that they would be renting the property out again directly. Steve asked them to keep in touch, and they agreed.

Shortly afterwards, Steve was contacted at his office by a woman who claimed to be psychic. "We're generally very skeptical of so-called psychics and mediums," he says. "We don't use them at MAPIT, and don't give them much credibility, frankly." But this woman claimed she had information about the

Foxholes Close house, and Steve decided to humor her out of curiosity. The psychic correctly told him that he'd been working on a case at a small house and that water was involved, but this revelation didn't impress him. She could have read the same newspaper article as everyone else had, after all. But then she went on to say that she kept seeing visions of a small, brown box buried in the back garden.

Steve didn't place much stock in her "visions," but on a lark, and in the interest of thoroughness, he contacted the council again. "Would you object to us having a dig around in the back garden?" he asked.

Council representatives had no objections, as the house was still empty. "Why?" they wanted to know.

"Oh, nothing really," Steve said. "We're just checking for an artifact that might have been left there." The council gave their approval. So one day, Steve and two of his investigators were back out at the Foxholes Close house with spades in hand. They spent the entire day plowing up the back garden, but found nothing at all. Steve's skepticism of psychics vindicated, he finally put the case to rest.

The data on Rochdale was put together and filed away. MAPIT received no further phone calls from Jim or Vera, and it was assumed that they spent the rest of their lives quietly, with no more incursions of the paranormal. The council contacted MAPIT from time to time. New residents reported nothing unusual about the house in Foxholes Close, though the team were called out on several occasions to investigate disturbances at some of the council's other properties. None of these, however, even approached the extent of the phenomena seen at the Gardner home.

Much later, MAPIT first went public with the case of the Rochdale Poltergeist. Media attention was immediate, intense, and worldwide. Newspapers, magazines, and TV programs from several countries all wanted a piece of the story. Steve believes that the main reason for the media frenzy was the simple fact of the water analysis, which was one of the few pieces of solid, scientific evidence that had been gathered in a paranormal case and verified by a disinterested third party.

The circus surrounding the case lasted for four or five months, and then, as is usual, attention began to focus elsewhere. Steve and the team at MAPIT went back to their daily routine, forever changed by the startling and enigmatic occurrences at the little house in Foxholes Close.

CHAPTER TEN

One of the most fascinating aspects of the Rochdale case was the prevalent manifestation of water appearing suddenly and in areas where its emergence was seemingly impossible. While the occasional unexplained puddles of water occur in some poltergeist cases, the "indoor rain" variation is far rarer. However, there have been a few similar reports in the paranormal canon.

For example, in October of 1963, the Martin family of Methuen, Massachusetts claimed that they begun to notice damp patches emerging from the walls. Initially believing the spots to be caused by a plumbing problem, the family soon realized something else was going on when water began shooting randomly out of walls, sometimes to a distance of two feet, and sometimes accompanied by a popping sound "like a small caliber pistol being discharged." The water was sticky to the touch, and always ice cold.

As in the Rochdale case, the water soon drenched the furniture and carpets, and an investigation by the deputy fire chief was unable to determine any source for the water. The phenomena—which according to reports seemed confined to the water manifestations and didn't include any other typical poltergeist happenings such as moving objects—followed the family to a relative's home two times when they were forced to flee their house to escape the onslaught.

Like many cases, the phenomena gradually went away on their own, though to this day there is no rational explanation for what could have been causing freezing cold water to suddenly jet from the plaster walls all over the house. This case, known as the "Methuen Water Demon," was also unusual in that there were no adolescent children in the family to act as a focus, and reports don't seem to highlight any particular stresses or hardships occurring with the Martins that might have kicked off the activity.

A similar occurrence evidently took place at a home in Piotrkow, Poland in 1993. In their book *The Return of the Elusive Power*, Anna Ostrzycka and Marek Rymuszko document a case wherein water and other liquids would suddenly gush from the walls, doors, and ceilings, and would even sometimes splash outwards from the furniture and from various containers. Inspectors from the city water department were called, but could find no obvious cause. There was apparently another case in Poland that occurred around the same time—though it was far less documented—in which a little boy was evidently causing water to fall from the ceiling of the apartment he lived in with his parents, as well as from the ceilings of buses he happened to be riding in at the time.

Well-known demonologists Ed and Lorraine Warren also investigated a similar "water poltergeist" in Saugerties, New York in which most of the same phenomena occurred as in Rochdale. They documented their experiences in their 2010 recorded lecture, *Water Poltergeist and Spirits of the Woods.*

A better-known case of strange water manifestation is that of Don Decker, the focus of the 1983 case known as "The Stroudsburg Rain Man." Decker was a troubled 21-year-old man who received a weekend furlough from prison to attend the funeral of his allegedly abusive grandfather. After the funeral, Decker returned to the home of family friends Bob and Jeannie Kieffer, where he suddenly began to manifest very strange behavior. He reported seeing a vision of an old man wearing a crown in an upstairs bathroom, and sported unusual scratches on his arm. He also apparently made pots and pans rattle as he walked past them, and displayed fugue-like behavior that led the Kieffers to describe him as seeming "possessed."

Shortly thereafter, much like in the Rochdale case, it began to rain indoors. The rain seemed to drip from the walls and ceiling without any reasonable explanation. This bizarre phenomena was witnessed by the residents of the home he was staying in, as well as the owner of the house (who was called to determine if the downpour was caused by a plumbing problem), and by two police patrolmen who were called later that night. Witnesses claimed to have seen raindrops occasionally defying gravity by falling upwards or sideways.

Decker's eerie "talent" continued to occur when he returned to prison, where he could apparently make it rain heavily inside his cell. This manifestation of the phenomena was also witnessed by several people, including other prisoners, guards, and the prison warden. Decker would go into an apparent "trance" when the rain was falling, and the room would reportedly get very cold. As in the Methuen case (but not in Rochdale), the water Decker apparently produced was sticky or oily to the touch.

In their book *The Rough Guide to Unexplained Phenomena: Mysteries and Curiosities of Science, Folklore and Superstition*, John Michell and Bob Rickard dedicate part of a chapter to documenting mysterious rainfalls and water manifestations. Many of the events described took place outside, albeit under unusual circumstances, but the authors do detail a few similar indoor water anomalies of the type that was present at Rochdale.

These include a case at a house in Eccleston, Lancashire, England in 1873, which featured torrents of water falling from the apparently dry ceilings, and an almost identical indoor rain that plagued the family living at an Ontario farm in 1880. Likewise, in 1919, a rectory in Norfolk, England was reported to have fallen victim to mysterious flows and spurting jets of liquid, which upon investigation proved to be a combination of paraffin and gasoline. Other collected liquids included water (on two occasions), alcohol, and sandalwood oil (on eleven occasions).

There was also the 1972 case of a hospitalized nine-year-old boy named Eugenio Rossi in Sardinia, who apparently caused puddles of water to ooze up through the floorboards around his bed. Hospital personnel witnessed this extraordinary occurrence, and proceeded to move the child to another ward, where the water promptly manifested again. The boy was moved to five different beds, but each time the oozing water returned. No explanation was ever found.

While manifestations of water are reported in far fewer cases than the standard rapping sounds and thrown objects, it seems clear that whatever mechanism causes so-called poltergeist phenomena can, in rare instances, display exceptionally bizarre behavior, including the apparently spontaneous manufacture of water and other substances. In none of the cases mentioned above was a rational cause for the liquids' appearance ever uncovered, despite efforts by plumbers, police, paranormal investigators, and others, and liquid manifestations of this type still remain an unusual and intriguing aspect of poltergeist activity.

AFTERWORD

As an interesting aside, as I was in the final stages of preparing this book for publication, it seemed that the Mammoth Mountain Poltergeist, as described in my first book along this line, returned for an encore performance, as though the simple discussion of paranormal phenomena triggered something that had apparently lay dormant for more than thirty years.

In the house I share with Tom in central Florida, two anomalous incidents occurred near the beginning of September 2015. The first took place on Friday, September 4th. I was not at home at the time, but Tom and other witnesses described what had happened. After a brief argument with his mother, Tom went into the master bedroom in a foul mood. Moments later, a loud crash from the kitchen drew Tom, his mother, and two visiting family friends out to investigate. It was soon determined that the lip of a shelf above the stove in the kitchen had somehow become detached and had caused two horse statues to plummet to the floor and shatter into pieces. The remaining two horse statues on the shelf remained in place.

At the time of the occurrence, Tom had not necessarily attributed it to paranormal phenomena, though he admitted the circumstances had been unusual. The statues that had broken, for example, had not been near enough to the edge of the shelf to have fallen off if the lip was removed; in addition, the lip had been nailed in place simply as a decorative and not functional element, and was not particularly loose. When he examined the lip of the shelf before nailing it back into place, he also noticed that the nails were bent strangely, as though the strip of wood had been pulled away from the shelf with great force.

Tom did not think much of this incident until another bizarre event occurred two days later. This incident was witnessed by Tom, myself, Tom's mother, and two friends who were visiting for the evening. The five of us were gathered in the living room, attempting to purchase a movie with our notoriously finicky satellite system. Much frustration ensued as the movie failed to start, and customer service were called. As the five of us sat arrayed around the room—Tom and me on one sofa, our friends on the other sofa perpendicular to us, and Tom's mother seated on a large ottoman across from us—the satellite remote, which had been sitting in the middle of the glass coffee table along with three other remotes, quite suddenly flew off the table and landed face down on the carpet about three feet away from its point of origin. It did not bounce as it landed, and made a decisive thud, as though the floor was magnetic and had attracted the object to it.

Everyone but Tom—who had been staring at a spot on the floor at the side of the sofa—witnessed its movement, and Tom observed it out of the corner of his eye, as a black blur. Much excitement ensued, as everyone assured each other that they had indeed seen the remote control inexplicably shoot off the table. No one had kicked or otherwise moved the table, and it was determined that the remote had been in the center of the wide table, and not teetering on the edge. The other three remotes did not move from their places, though Tom thinks he may have seen them move very slightly in his peripheral vision. The five of us picked up the remote and tried to replicate its motion by simply dropping it from the table's edge. This inevitably produced a bouncing motion, and a clicking sound quite unlike the thud it had made the first time. It also traveled no more than a foot or so.

At this point, Tom admitted that his hair was standing on end, just as it had quite often when paranormal incidents were taking place during his 1982 experience. As the five of us were discussing the event and trying to rationalize how it could have happened, we noticed that a quarter had appeared on the carpet, roughly in the spot where Tom had been staring when the remote left the table. Though this was a rather ambiguous incident, all present insisted that there had not been a quarter there before, and no one could determine where the coin could have come from.

After those two incidents, the house fell quiet once again. Tom told me that he made a deliberate decision to downplay the events, both in his own mind and to others, in order to ensure that the phenomena would not escalate the way it did in 1982, when he was a frightened, high-strung teenager. As a skeptic, and as the author of now two books describing ostensibly real poltergeist phenomena, I am edified that I finally got to be able to witness a tiny fraction of the manifestations myself.

BIBLIOGRAPHY & SUGGESTED READING

"Anomalous Rain or Water Out Of Nowhere." *Anomalous Rain or Water Out Of Nowhere*. N.p., n.d. Web. 23 Sept. 2015.

Ashford, Jenny, and Tom Ross. *The Mammoth Mountain Poltergeist*. N.p.: CreateSpace, 2015. Print.

Clarkson, Michael. *The Poltergeist Phenomenon: An In-depth Investigation into Floating Beds, Smashing Glass, and Other Unexplained Disturbances*. Pompton Plains, NJ: New Page, 2011. Print.

"Don Decker - The Rain Man Poltergeist." *Historic Mysteries*. N.p., 20 Aug. 2013. Web. 23 Sept. 2015.

"Ghosts, Hauntings, Legends and Old Odd Tales of Lancashire." *Ghosts, Hauntings, Legends and Old Odd Tales of Lancashire*. N.p., n.d. Web. 23 Sept. 2015.

Henderson, Jan-Andrew. *The Ghost That Haunted Itself: The Story of the McKenzie Poltergeist*. Edinburgh: Mainstream, 2001. Print.

Hines, Terence. *Pseudoscience and the Paranormal*. Amherst, NY: Prometheus, 2003. Print.

Houran, James, and Rense Lange. *Hauntings and Poltergeists. Multidisciplinary Perspectives*. N.p.: McFarland, 2007. Print.

Imich, Alexander. "High Strangeness: Water Poltergeists." *High Strangeness: Water Poltergeists*. N.p., n.d. Web. 23 Sept. 2015.

"Interviews with Steve Mera." Online interview. 25 Apr. 2015.

"Interviews with Steve Mera." Online interview. 27 Apr. 2015.

"Interviews with Steve Mera." Online interview. 28 Apr. 2015.

"MAPIT." *Welcome -*. N.p., n.d. Web. 23 Sept. 2015.

Mera, Steve. "My Biggest Fright!" *Keeping the Paranormal Friendly*, 18 Apr. 2012. Web. 23 Sept. 2015.

Michell, John, and Robert J. M. Rickard. "Mysterious Flows and Oozings." *Unexplained Phenomena: A Rough Guide Special*. London: Rough Guides, 2000. 51-54. Print.

Nicholls, Robert (2004). *Curiosities of Greater Manchester*. Sutton Publishing. ISBN 0-7509-3661-4.

Nickell, Joe. "Enfield Poltergeist, Investigative Files". August 2012. *Committee for Skeptical Inquiry*. Retrieved 3 December 2013.

Ostrzycka, Anna, and Marek Rymuszko. *The Return of the Elusive Power*. Warsaw: Phenomen, 1994. Print.

"Paranormal Skeptic Rains on Stroudsburg's Devil Tale." *Poconorecord.com*. N.p., n.d. Web. 23 Sept. 2015.

Playfair, Guy Lyon. *This House Is Haunted: The Amazing inside Story of the Enfield Poltergeist*. Guildford: White Crow, 2011. Print.

"Poltergeist." *Poltergeist*. N.p., n.d. Web. 23 Sept. 2015.

"Rochdale Haunted House." *YouTube*. YouTube, n.d. Web. 23 Sept. 2015.

"Rochdale Poltergeist." *MAPIT*. N.p., n.d. Web. 23 Sept. 2015.

"Steve Mera Bio." *The Phenomena Project*. N.p., n.d. Web. 23 Sept. 2015.

Wagner, Stephen. "Water, Water Everywhere... From Nowhere." N.p., n.d. Web. 23 Sept. 2015.

Water Poltergeist and Spirits of the Woods. Perf. Ed Warren and Lorraine Warren. Omnimedia Publishing LLC, 2010. DVD.

ABOUT THE AUTHORS

Jenny Ashford is a horror writer and graphic artist. Her other books include *Red Menace*, *Bellwether*, *The Five Poisons*, *The Tenebrist*, and two short-story collections, *Hopeful Monsters* and *The Associated Villainies*. She has also written a paranormal nonfiction account titled *The Mammoth Mountain Poltergeist* with Tom Ross. Her short stories have appeared in anthologies including *The Nightmare Collective*, *History Is Dead*, *2012 AD*, *ChimeraWorld #3* and *ChimeraWorld #4*. Her horror blog, goddessofhellfire.com, contains current writing news, short stories and articles, and her opinions about horror films and the genre in general.

Steve Mera is a parapsychologist, paranormal investigator, freelance journalist, lecturer and tutor. He is the owner of the free monthly publication known as *Phenomena Magazine*, and chairman and founder of the Scientific Establishment of Parapsychology in Manchester, England. He is the author of three books—*Strange Happenings: Memoirs of a Paranormal Investigator; Paranormal Insight: A Concise Study of the Strange and Profound*; and *The Paranormal Investigators Handbook: A Professional Look at the Subject of Ghosthunting*. He has appeared on over 90 TV shows and series, over 100 radio stations, and has published articles in over 300 publications internationally.